Alexander Means

A Cluster of Poems

For the Home and the Heart

Alexander Means

A Cluster of Poems
For the Home and the Heart

ISBN/EAN: 9783744665582

Printed in Europe, USA, Canada, Australia, Japan

Cover: Foto ©Thomas Meinert / pixelio.de

More available books at **www.hansebooks.com**

A CLUSTER OF POEMS,

FOR THE

HOME AND THE HEART,

GATHERED BY THE AUTHOR AT LEISURE HOURS.

From Nature's gorgeous expanse
Around him,
Her shining worlds
Above him,

Her glowing deeps
Below him,
And from her whispering galleries
Within him.

BY
REV. A. MEANS, D. D., LL. D.
EMORY COLLEGE, OXFORD, GA., 1878.

NEW YORK:
E. J. HALE & SON, PUBLISHERS,
MURRAY STREET.
1878.

Entered according to Act of Congress
  By Rev. A. Means, D. D.,
In the office of the Librarian of Congress

STEREOTYPED AND PRINTED
BY THE
NATIONAL PRINTING CO.,
13 CHAMBERS STREET,
NEW YORK.

DEDICATION.

PROMPTED BY A LONG-STANDING PERSONAL ATTACHMENT,

AND BY

VIVID MEMORIES OF THE "AULD LANG SYNE;"

AS WELL AS BY A HIGH ESTIMATE OF

THE MAN, THE MINISTER, and THE BISHOP,

THIS LITTLE VOLUME IS

RESPECTFULLY DEDICATED BY THE AUTHOR,

TO THE

REV. GEORGE F. PIERCE, D.D., LL.D.,
BISHOP OF THE METHODIST EPISCOPAL CHURCH SOUTH.

Preface.

THESE poetic effusions are the products of leisure hours, gained, through many years past, from the pursuit of heavier and more imperative duties, and are now respectfully and deferentially submitted to the public, at the repeated requests of many friends. Among them will be found Epic, Lyric, and Elegiac Poems, with Sacred Melodies, Sunday School Odes, and a few compositions, designed, when written, as Ministerial Solos, for public and special occasions, and at a time when this element of public worship was more frequently employed than at the present day.

It will be seen that the author has not thought it advisable to arrange and classify these different styles of poetic composition under the several heads to which they may technically belong, but has largely distributed them throughout the volume, as likely to afford the consecutive reader a more agreeable variety than he might expect to enjoy by a methodical aggroupment of each different species of poetry. They are thus presented, then, with the sincere wish and ardent hope, that amid the diversity of themes which they embrace, they may, at least in some slight degree, contribute to please, cheer, and elevate some minds, and excite pure and sublime emotions in some hearts.

In conclusion: as the writer has, from boyhood, ever honored and esteemed the sex of his *mother*, he may be allowed to add, that he has sought to throw a sanctity and loveliness around the character of *woman*—to spring within her new aspirations for a still nobler position in society upon earth, and to charm her with the claims and awards of heaven.

Such as the contents of this volume are, however, they are humbly consecrated to the cause of God and humanity.

Introduction.

THE author of this volume of poems was born in Statesville, North Carolina, February 6th, 1801. From early manhood to this day, he has been among the busiest and best workers of his time. He became a student of necessity; for from early boyhood he "hungered and thirsted" after truth. Thorough elemental training laid a good foundation for the noble superstructure of varied and useful learning which even now, while "the almond tree flourishes," employs his energies; for such a man, though realizing that he can never finish in this world the work God gives him to do, must keep ever in his heart that word of the Master: "Occupy till I come."

In medicine, science, literature, and theology, our honored friend has been, without intermission of zeal, an enthusiastic, painstaking student. As physician, scientist, writer, and preacher, he holds an honorable place among his contemporaries. For nearly half a century he has been identified with the great interests of education. Thousands throughout the South still live to bless him for the lessons learned in his class and lecture rooms.

The vauntings of atheistic science bring no alarms to his steadfast heart. He has learned, for himself, that "God in nature and God in revelation are one." He hails with delight all real discoveries in science, and claims them as trophies for his King and Saviour. He believes, with great-hearted Milton, that "Truth, in some age or other, will find her witness, and shall be justified at last by her own children."

Intimate knowledge of our author naturally reminds one of Lord Bacon's wise saying: "It is true that a little philosophy inclineth man's mind to atheism, but depth in philosophy bringeth men's minds about to religion: for while the mind of man looketh upon second causes scattered, it may sometimes rest in them, and go no farther; but when it beholdeth the chain of them, confederate and linked together, it must needs fly to Providence and Deity."

A man who studies God and nature with a heart so susceptible and a spirit so reverent, must sometimes find himself "soaring in the high regions of his fancy, with his garland and singing robes about him." In the world around him and in the heavens above him he must see what others do not see, and hear what others do not hear, being among those favored ones

> "Who carry music in their heart
> Through dusky lane and wrangling mart;
> Plying their daily task with busier feet,
> Because their secret souls a holier strain repeat."

Very truly do the wise Germans say: "In this world the eye sees what it brings capacity for seeing." A thousand times, as these poems are witness, our friend has felt in his heart of hearts all that Coleridge sings in his "Morning Hymn in the Vale of Chamouni:"

> "Awake, my soul! Not only passive praise
> Thou owest! Not alone these swelling tears,
> Mute thanks and secret ecstasy! Awake,
> Voice of sweet song! Awake, my heart, awake!
> Green vales and icy cliffs, join in my hymn!"

In this dainty little volume are many songs of the affections. Our author has modestly named them "A Cluster of Poems for the Home and the Heart." And they are well named, since he is one of the happy men who can sing with Croly of "Domestic Love:"

> "Oh love of loves! to thy white hand is given
> Of earthly happiness the golden key;
> Thine are the joyous hours of winter's even,
> When the babes cling around their father's knee,
> And thine the voice that on the midnight sea,
> Meets the rude mariner with thoughts of home,
> Peopling the gloom with all he longs to see."

This volume has been demanded of its author by a host of friends, and most earnestly by his old students. There are thousands, in his own section, many in the Northern and Western States of our great Union, and some across the water, who will be glad to see and to enjoy this "Cluster of Poems for the Home and the Heart." And they may welcome it without fear; for there is not one poisonous flower in the cluster. There is not a line in this book that will bring a shadow to any home, a blush to any cheek, a snare to any heart.

ATTICUS G. HAYGOOD.

EMORY COLLEGE,
OXFORD, GA., *Dec.* 25, 1877.

CONTENTS.

	PAGE
"All Shall be Well,"	55
An Epithalamium,	210
An Infant's Flight to Heaven,	167
Apostrophe to an Album,	145
Apostrophe to the Stone Mountain, An,	26
Appendix,	214
Atlanta Crushed and Crowned,	50
Balloon's Ascension, The,	81
Beauty Enhanced by Piety,	168
Camp-meeting Hymn,	200
Camp-meeting Song,	208
Capers, Little Charles Meminger, Elegy on,	102
Chamouni, Vale of,	11
Christian Sabbath, The,	36
Conviction and Conversion Contrasted,	128
Cupboard, The Little Pine, &c.,	151
Deluge, The Noachian,	83
Emory and Oxford Apostrophized,	144
Farewell and the Greeting, The,	157
Farewell Souvenir, A,	133
Ffriendship's Memorial,	174
Ffrown of God, The,	48
Girlhood Expanded to Womanhood,	182
Glacier in the Heart, A,	149
Gloom and Glory,	128
Golden Girdle, The,	177
Golden Wedding, The,	210
Grandeur of Nature and the Glory of Grace, Contrasted,	112
Itinerant Minister's Wife, To an,	166
Ladies' Welcome, The,	119
"Little Ones, My Little Ones,"	193
"Live for the Skies,"	200
Madrigal, A,	181
Masonic Ode, A,	78
Means, Miss Sallie L., Sketch of the late,	135
Messiah's Coming Reign,	188

CONTENTS.

	Page
Millennium, A Vision of the,	16
Minister's Farewell, The,	191
Morning in May, A,	169
Mount of Holiness, The,	78
New Year's Reflections—1866—A,	110
Ode to the Opening of the New Year, 1860,	31
Parental Affection,	206
Phases of Woman, The,	29
Pine Cupboard, The Little, &c.,	151
Pledge of Affection, A,	180
Poetic Offering, A,	140
Poetic Paraphrase of the Forty-eighth Psalm,	184
Purity Rewarded,	77
Rainbow Dream, The,	23
Reminiscence (for his Wife) A,	80
Sabbath, The Christian,	36
Sacred Localities in Palestine,	95
Samford, T. P., A Tribute to the memory of,	58
Silent Power of Woman, The,	147
Song-bird Uncaged, The,	100
Souvenir, A Farewell,	133
Souvenir of Love, A,	117
Sparkling Beauty Transient,	205
"Sunday-school, Our Sunday-school,"	197
Supplement to "The War,"	69
The Sear Leaf,	171
The Sound of the Gospel is Passing Away,	202
The Train,	72
The War, and one of its Noble Victims,	58
To the Author's Eldest Daughter,	206
Tribute of Gratitude, A,	114
Tribute to the Heroic Dead,	108
Triumphant Wife and Mother, A,	163
Triumph of a Lofty Faith in Woman, The,	130
Triumph of Joseph,	77
Vision of the Millennium, A,	16
Vale of Chamouni, in the Swiss Alps,	11
Wedding Ring, The,	207
Woman in Paradise, and Woman in Christendom,	122
Woman, Silent Power of,	147
Woman, Triumph of a Lofty Faith in,	130
World Without, and the World Within, The,	105
Young Student's Cloudless Close of Life, The,	186
Young Womanhood Ripe for Heaven,	135

A CLUSTER OF POEMS.

The Vale of Chamouni,

IN THE SWISS ALPS.

WRITTEN AFTER WITNESSING THE SUBLIME SCENES OF THAT MOUNTAIN REGION.

Sweet Vale of Chamouni! the "Pride of the Mountains,"
   Thou bloomest in beauty, high up in the skies;
Where the roar of bright cascades from wild, gushing fountains,
   A torrent of music forever supplies.

The Aiguille de Rouges rise in grandeur around thee,
   Encinctur'd with jasper and crested with snow;
To loom o'er the nestling retreat where I found thee,
   And cast their deep shadow o'er gorges below.

High, high to the eastward, to shut out the morning,
　The bold Montanvert rears its turreted steeps;
The ice-wreaths of winter their summits adorning,
　Far aloft from the crags whence the avalanche leaps.

Upheav'd from thy plain, and defying the ages—
　His time-honor'd diadem bare to the sky;
His body-guards round him, where bleak winter rages—
　The " Monarch of Mountains," MONT BLANC, meets the eye.

Great Castle of Nature! Thy pinnacles tower
　Columnar and grand, and transpiercing the clouds,
Where Jupiter Tonans ne'er hazards his power,
　But stoops to the zone which his storm-cloud enshrouds.

Hark! hark! how it thunders!—the mountains are quaking!
　The *tread of an avalanche* sounds on the gale!
Vast bowlders are bounding! the forest is breaking!
　Whole hamlets and herds are entomb'd in the vale!

Great God! when the Alpine artill'ry's unlimber'd,
   And cloud-mounted caissons supply the death-balls;
When the cannonade rolls over ice-fields, untimber'd,
   Woe! woe to the homes where the thunder-shock falls!

*   *   *   *   *   *

Yonder—stretching in gelid and motionless splendor,
   Through a half hundred miles—lies the cold Mer de Glace;
For deep mountain gorges their basins surrender,
   To cradle for ages the huge frozen mass.

With margins of azure, its yawning crevasses
   Pierce down fifty fathoms — chill, gloomy, and dread,
As if cleft by the lightnings, to open the passes
   To Pluto's dark caves, and their shadowy dead.

Fronting far to the west, and in splendent illusion,
   The Glacier du Bois lifts its arch of sea-green;
Whence the Arviron leaps from its icy seclusion,[*]
   Uncavern'd and free, to give life to the scene.

---

[*] A subterraneous stream which gushes out from the western base of the glacier.

The Arve, rushing by, claims the fugitive stranger,
  And bursts every barrier, to blend with the Rhone;
While dark frowning cliffs overhang it with danger,
  Nor heed its wild wail through its channels of stone.

Lash'd on by the Furies that rul'd at its fountains,
  In headlong persistence—defiant of foes—
It clears rocky ledges, tears open the mountains,
  And roars with the tempest, the wilder it blows.

But the Rhone is in sight! and these ostracised daughters—
  A blonde and brunette, in discordant embrace*—
Soon close their career in Geneva's blue waters,
  Their rest to secure, and their stains to efface.†

Here, plung'd and absterg'd by their azure lavation,
  In beauty and loveliness now they agree;
And silently seeking a new destination,
  Their sweet limpid waters glide on to the sea.

Bright type of the soul as it enters probation!
  Polluted and restless through life to be driv'n,

---

*Appendix A.   †Appendix B.

Until, wash'd in the laver of regeneration,
  Its purified essence flows smoothly to heav'n.

I knew, fair Chamouni! that rock-ramparts bound thee,
  And Titans, ice-thron'd, have conspir'd to destroy;
But Phœbus shall smite them—green glories surround thee—
  And spring-time and summer then crown thee with joy.

Farewell, cloister'd Eden! I leave thee forever!
  No more through thy gorges and glaciers to roam;
But in far distant lands I'll forget, never, never,
  The grandeur and peace of thy sweet mountain home.

A Vision of the Millennium.

A PRIZE POEM.*

Away! away! my restless, reaching mind!
Obey the impulse, beating high within—
The truthful index of immortal life.
Away from books and banks and civil strife,
And all the horde of mercenary cares,
Long, long taskmasters o'er thy humbled powers.

Let nobler themes, reveal'd to mortal ken,
Arouse thy slumb'ring energies t' ascend
The empyrean arch which grandly spans
Ethereal regions, flush'd with glowing life;—
And foll'wing far the onward lines of light
That richly streak the cloudless moral heavens
And make their focus on a distant age,
O'erleap the lapse of intervening years,
And settle down beneath the hemisphere

---

* A premium granted.

Of uncreated light that pales the stars,
And canopies the globe with dazzling sheen—
Surpassing far yon zone of ample sweep
That belts the evening sky of Saturn's orb.

Transcendent light of God's millennial day!
The hallow'd radiance of supernal bliss!
The end of prophecy! The reign of Heav'n!

To this, in bygone years, the holy seers
With gifted vision look'd; and patriarchs,
And saints of later age, all bent their eyes
Upon the looming future, full of hope.
The gath'ring light of eighteen hundred years
Has half reveal'd the soul-absorbing scene,
And sprung the faith of Zion's sons afresh.

Earth, air and sea, their noblest tribute pay,
To speed creation to its goal of bliss.
Immortal mind is levied on from high,
And plumes her wing for bold empyreal flight.
E'en Mammon smiles, and taps his golden stores,
To cheer the heathen with the "Book of Life;"
While Science, thron'd amid the starry hosts,
And wielding far the scepter of her reign

O'er boundless realms—her own—sublimely bows,
And wreaths her wealth of honors round the Cross.

   The Arts—her servants all—submissive yield
Their gen'rous tribute to the glorious work;
And rivaling in speed the panting winds,
Her wondrous messengers, on burning wheel
Swift scour the bosom of the boiling seas,
And bear on board the commerce of the world;
Nay, rarer still, the pabulum of life,
In Bible stores, to feed its famish'd tribes.
Then, rushing on o'er continental plains,
They bound in smoke and thunder through the hills,
And tunnel'd mountains echo to their tread,
As, drap'd in night, and yelling to the winds,
They pierce th' embowel'd rock, and, belching fire,
Insult his throne, and challenge Pluto's reign!
The Stygian gloom surpass'd, th' emergent train
Swings high in air, and rings along the cliffs;
Transilient, clears a hundred yawning chasms,
And, tireless, leaps the intervening floods,
To hail with eagle scream the farthest goal.

   Not still enough to crown this matchless age,
And conquer Nature for the reign of Grace—

The very seas unbar their coral caves,
To let the world look in! And far below
The em'rald beds where fabled mermaids sleep,
The wir'y cable springs its graceful curves,
And widely spans suboceanic steeps;
While thought, electric, shoots the deeps profound,
To gladden nations on the distant shore,
And bind, in brothers' bonds, antipodes.

All, all portend th' august, approaching day.
Faith, stirr'd by thick'ning signs that mark the time,
Uplifts her kindling eye, and hurries on
To hail the dawn of great Messiah's reign.

The world's foregone! Its noisy din is hush'd;
Earth's sickly hopes and vapid joys forgot.
The orient heav'ns, aglow with liquid gold,
Outspread their splendors on creation's hosts.

The wid'ning day unfolds—THE SHILOH COMES!
The streamers from His rising throne flash far,
And flush the skies with greater glories near.

Hail! Prince of Peace! Great David's Son and Lord!

Eternal Power, all hail! Forever hail!
The ransom'd nations shout, "Thy kingdom come!"

* * * * *

Oh, what a scene! A God on earth again!
And crowding millions of apostate men,
Each full of heaven, and welcom'd to His smiles!
Symphonious hallelujahs echoing far,
And rolling on the winds, to list'ning zones,
The boundless raptures of a world redeem'd!

All, all is peace. Perennial glory shines
O'er the broad bosom of the moral deep.
No ruffian tempests lash the sea of life,
To wreck their victims on a hopeless coast;
Calm sleep the waves—the howling winds are hush'd,
For more than Neptune rules the noiseless main.
Thrice hallow'd era to the tribes of earth!
The great Deceiver struggles in his chains,
The prison'd victim of Messiah's pow'r.
Infernal malice heaves its burning breast,
But dare not sluice its venom on the world.
Sin, scath'd and sear'd, has wither'd to its death,
And plants of holy growth o'erspread the land.
No clarion rings t' inflame the martial'd host,
Or drown the clangor of their flashing steel;

No thund'ring ordnance shakes th' ensanguin'd plain,
Nor butcher'd thousands bleach on foreign soil.
No deadly blade is launch'd by villain's hand;
No reckless mobs exult in seething flames.
The black, confounded brotherhood of crime
Abhor the light, and covert seek in hell.
One broad, one boundless, one intensive day
Illumes the moral world, and gilds the grave!
Earth breathes the air of heaven. Celestial sounds
Ring through her thousand palaces, and swell
In rapturous strains from cottages of clay!

One step—one brief, one rapid, noiseless step,
Soft as an angel's tread on Hermon's dew—
And all is heaven; unmask'd, unclouded *heaven!*
A God UNVEIL'D! Supernal bliss begun.
Stupendous thought! The ravish'd soul's o'erwhelm'd!
Its seat a throne; immensity its range!

* * * * * *

But stay! These vasty contemplations sweep
My spirit from its moorings. Where am I?
High heaven's the focus of the Godhead's light,
Where none but eyes immortal gaze unscath'd.

* * * * * *

Poor earth-born child, retreat! Thou tread'st too far;
Thy sense o'erpower'd recoils, and shrinks abash'd.

Await the opening future fast in *faith*,
And, clad in peerless mail of heav'nly mold,
Still breast the wingless bolts that wand'ring fly
From spent assailants, tott'ring to their fall.

A mother's voice inspires, and sainted forms
That arm'd thy boyhood with the shield of pray'r,
Seem bending from their thrones of living light,
And wave the victor's palm, to woo thee on.

The conflict nears its close—the heights are scal'd—
The fiercest batt'ries, silenc'd, boom no more.
Th' infernal foe, with shatter'd shield and blade,
Vindictive, fears and flies supernal pow'r,
And leaves his strongholds to the " sons of God."

The skies are blushing as the morning rose;
And Vict'ry, bending from her azure throne,
Entwines her garlands for Thy conq'ring brow.
Thy rapturous gaze, from inspiration's peaks,
Caught but the adumbration, shooting far,
Of world-wide splendors in a coming age.
That age is hast'ning on. God speed its pace,
Till, stooping from their heights, the burthen'd skies
Are rent with overcharge of endless bliss,
And cloudless glory merges earth in heaven!

The Rainbow Dream.

A PREMIUM POEM.*

It was night on the plain, and the village was still;
   Not a wing was afloat on the air.
Ev'ry wheel was at rest in the neighboring mill,
   And the invalid doz'd in his chair.

I had pray'd for the lov'd ones in camps far away,
   And had sunk in the arms of repose,
Overpower'd by the cares and the toils of the day,
   When a bright dreamy vision arose.

It was twilight, it seem'd, as I gaz'd from my room,
   And beheld, in the dark southern sky,
A RAINBOW in beauty and majesty loom
   O'er the billowy cloud-drifts on high.

As I stepp'd from the door, and with rapid eye-glance
   Swept the broad panorama around,

---

* Written during the war, and truthful in its details.

How sublime was the pomp through the blazing expanse!
    While the atmosphere breath'd not a sound.

For in prismatic glory the heavens all smil'd,
    And shone on the landscape below;
From horizon to zenith the arches were pil'd—
    East, west, north and south were aglow!

Fleecy masses of vapor, disrupted and pale,
    As if taking their leave of the sky,
Floated gloomily by over mountain and vale—
    Yet they robb'd not a bow of its dye.

Far aloft in the east was the "All-seeing Eye,"
    And, resplendent with streamers of light,
It was burning like Constantine's Cross in the sky,
    While the world stood in awe at the sight.

Great God! with what grandeur creation then shone,
    In her purple, and crimson, and gold!
Was the curtain uplifted that circles the Throne,
    And a scroll from the Godhead unroll'd?

Were the thousand bright arches that spann'd the
    blue dome,
  The symbolic foretokens of peace?
Shall the tempest that beats o'er my once happy
    home,
  And the thunder of battle, soon cease?

Shall the red clouds of war, rent and torn by the
    blast
  That Mercy shall speed from on high,
Be swept from our sky, and the sunshine at last
  Kindle joy through the land, far and nigh?

Does the eye of Omniscience auspiciously beam
  On the land of the orange and pine,
To encourage our faith with the glories that gleam
  From a providence truly divine?

Then thanks for the vision, so rich and so rare,
  So abounding with hope and with God!
We shall outlive the tempest, and breathe a free air,
  Where ensanguin'd battalions have trod!

An Apostrophe to the Stone Mountain.*

SITUATED IN DE KALB COUNTY, GEORGIA.

Great granite monster, whence thy birth?
   What age upheav'd thy giant form?
Why has the rent and lab'ring earth
   Disgorg'd thee bare to sun and storm?

Why cling'st thou to her breast, disown'd—
   A naked outcast, scath'd and peel'd—
While smiling plains her lap has nurs'd,
   Are crown'd with wealth of wood and field?

A foundling flung, without a name,
   'Mid winds and skies to stand alone;
What paps have nurs'd thy Titan frame?
   What gorgon glance transform'd to stone?

Thy natal hour no mem'ries reach—
   Far lost in a primeval age,

---

* See Appendix O.

When fire and flood, in fearful breach
    Of pristine order, shot their rage.

Upheav'd to heaven, in hoary pride,
    O'er toppling thrones thou tow'rest now.
Wild hurricanes have lash'd thy side;
    Insulting thunders storm'd thy brow.

Yet there thou gloomest, stern and strong—
    The wrecks of tempests at thy feet;
The storm-god's thrilling battle-gong
    Silenc'd, as all his hosts retreat.

Bald, bleak and bleach'd, thou ling'rest on,
    Survivor of a world entomb'd;
And, rob'd in light, thy rocky throne
    Shall brave the skies till earth is doom'd.

Great monumental pile, live on!
    For suns shall gild thy royal head
When Egypt's pyramids are gone,
    With all their underlying dead.

Down deep below thy cloudless face
    The storm of internecine war

May roll its columns round thy base,
    Led on by their portentous star.

Unsheeted heroes long shall sleep
    In countless thousands at thy feet,
And widows wail, and orphans weep,
    No more their mold'ring dead to greet.*

But though a people gor'd and torn,
    Bewail in blood their martyrs gone—
No grief for millions thus that mourn,
    Shall ever stir thy heart of stone.

In scathless strength and stoic gloom,
    Thou still shalt mock the wastes of years,
Till herald thunders wake the tomb,
    And God in judgment pomp appears.

---

*During the late destructive war between the Northern and Southern States, a battle was fought near the base of this mountain.

The Phases of Woman.

I saw her a bright and a lovely thing,
    As she press'd the lips that taught her;
Like a rosebud nurs'd in the lap of spring
    She bloom'd—and I call'd her "daughter."

Again I gaz'd as she pass'd along,
    And a brother smil'd and kiss'd her;
With her ringing laugh and her witching song,
    'Twas a joy to call her "sister."

I saw her again in her queenly pride,
    As a raptur'd lover claim'd her;
She stood at the altar, his brilliant bride,
    And his charming "wife" he nam'd her.

I saw her a matron, in riper years,
    When she clasp'd to her heart another;
It lay and gaz'd on her grateful tears;
    Then smil'd, and call'd her "mother."

I saw her last, as she pass'd away,
    With her household bending round her;
A convoy came from the realms of day,
    And an "angel" form they found her.

Oh, let me repose upon woman's breast!
    Let her lap in childhood hold me!
And in ripe old age, when I sink to rest,
    May her guardian arms enfold me!

An Ode to the Opening of the New Year, 1860;

THE EVE OF OUR CALAMITOUS WAR.

How placidly shines the morning star,
   As she starts on her new career;
And heralds the pomp of Aurora's car,
   Through the gates of the opening year!

In advance of the rosy blush of day,
   She moves as a virgin queen;
And ascends the skies but to sink away
   In the depths of their blue serene.

The orient heavens are pav'd with gold,
   For the tread of Apollo's wheel;
And its dazzling beams, as the gates unfold,
   An awaking world reveal.

The homes of the happy with shouts resound,
   As they welcome the new-born cheer;

While *Eighteen Hundred and Sixty's* crown'd,
  And hail'd as the reigning year.

The morning has spread her silver sheen
  On the mountain's glowing brow,
And millions that greet the resplendent scene
  Now start to the loom and plow.

How merrily rings the peasant's song
  O'er his sunlit hills and plains;
While maids and mothers the notes prolong,
  Until childhood swells the strains.

But the laugh and the sport of the "Christmas-tree,"
  And the "Christmas-gift" and gun,
With the negro's smirk, and his banjo glee,
  Have fled from the rising sun;

While a thousand wheels that have palsied hung
  Till the holiday sports were o'er,
Are now in their bands and braces swung,
  And thunder and smoke once more.

Then away, away as their echoes roll
  Over mountain and lake and field,

Lo! the nations are rousing from Line to Pole,
    For the shock of the spear and shield.

There's a struggle ahead, 'twixt counter pow'rs,
    And the thrones of the kingdoms shake;
The heavens are gath'ring avenging show'rs,
    And the hearts of the guilty quake.*

Oh, ye godly seers of the filmy past!
    Ere the midsummer sign shall rise,
Shall my country stoop to the stormy blast,
    Or withstand the inclement skies?

Great Power above! lock the demon's wheel
    That rushes with blade and brand
To gloat o'er the carnage of crimson'd steel,
    And the smoke of a burning land!

A fratricide's doom is in red reserve,
    And Vengeance has nurs'd the blaze,
To scathe and to scar the vandal nerve
    That essays the torch to raise.

Oh, bind our temple with bolts of steel,
    And seam it with molten gold!

---

* There were at this time rumors of war in Europe.

From its flaming walls let the traitor reel,
    Under Julian's curse of old!

But surely a cordon of angels stand
    To encircle its lofty dome;
And a legion more, by divine command,
    Shall encamp round Freedom's home.

Then bury the past in eternal night,
    With its tales, and tears, and blood;
Let us rise on the wings of the morning's light,
    To meet and commune with God.

Though creation's clock no sound has rung,
    And its beat has alarm'd no ears;
Yet are countless cycles of ages flung
    From the sweep of its rolling spheres.

We are onward bound, with a brisker breeze
    And a bolder piston stroke;
Already we rock on the heaving seas,
    And the favoring skies invoke.

There are signs in the heavens, and signs on earth,
    That presage the millennial reign;

And millions of prayers, of priceless worth,
    Are ascending from land and main.

The Lion of Judah has open'd the seal,
    And the last seventh trumpet sounds;
Like Alpine thunder, the echoing peal
    From the temple of God resounds.

O God of the cross to the guilty giv'n!
    In thy cloudless reign appear;
Make the earth an elysium fill'd with heaven,
    Ere the close of this circling year!

The Christian Sabbath:

LIKE POPE'S BRITISH ROSE, "THE TYPE OF SWEET RULE AND GENTLE MAJESTY."

ANALYSIS. — *1. Its antiquity and continuance a proof of its divine origin. 2. Dawn of day. 3. Sunrise. 4. Its universal quiet, and noiseless reign. 5. The morning Sunday-school. 6. Approaching noon. 7. Gathering to the house of worship. 8. Church service commenced. 9. The pulpit appeal of the hour. 10. Its solemn and affecting close. 11. A more extended survey. 12. The Sabbath on a heathen shore. 13. The Missionary's triumph. 14. The hallowing anticipation of the* ETERNAL SABBATH.

HAIL, peaceful Sabbath! Type of endless rest!
Thou voiceless oracle of priceless truth!
The nation's guarantee that Israel's God—
Who in the depth of by-gone years, from high,
Baptized thy virgin hours, and claim'd them His—
Still lives in Zion, stretching far His reign,
And pouring proof on prophecy, where'er
Thy hallow'd sunshine greets the Christian world!

Thrice welcome, happy day! my spirit hails
With joyous bound thy monumental hours.
They come, fresh with the story of the Cross,
And laden with salvation's richest fruits,

Ripéd on Calv'ry's top in noonday night,
And grown in luscious plenty from the soil
Steep'd in the gore of God's vicarious Son.

   Sweet day of rest! How still creation round!
Hush'd in divine repose; still more like heaven,
When starry sentinels with beamless lamps,
Retiring fast, throw wide the gates of day,
And o'er the waking millions, looming high,
Aurora's purple robe adorns the east—
Emblazon'd symbol of approaching pomp.
But soon, the portals past, in crimson glow
Apollo's blazing chariot mounts the sky,
And, slowly rolling up the steep of heaven,
In cloudless glory flings its golden light
In wide profusion over flood and field—
Now sporting on the slumb'ring infant's cheek,
And kissing into second life the lids
Late softly lock'd in soothing sleep's embrace;
And now, its dazzling luster flashing far
O'er dimpling stream and azure-tinted lake,
Wakes up the sleepers from their wat'ry beds,
And, bounding into light, the finny tribes
Leap high in air t' express their Maker's praise;
While woods, responsive to the glad'ning sounds,

Send back the echoes of a thousand strains
From joyous warblers in their leafy bow'rs,
Their matin melodies of grateful song.

But now creation's hymns have ceas'd, and wide
The blissful Sabbath spreads its balmy peace;
Intelligence is thron'd to honor God,
And hush the clamors of a guilty world.
*   *   *   *   *   *
Behold how wide the noiseless quiet reigns!
The plow mid-furrow stands, as loath to move,
And mar the solemn grandeur of the scene.
The faithful ox, half dozing 'mid the shade,
Revolves his cud, or freely roams the plain.
The noble horse, reliev'd from rein and draught,
His forage grinds, and, patient in his stall,
Atones in dreamy mood his weekly toils.
The grating saw, reverberating axe
And rustling plane, their deaf'ning stridor hush,
And noisy Commerce shuts her thousand doors.
The busy fact'ry's thund'rous hum has ceas'd—
Its glowing wheels have paus'd to take their rest;
Its prison'd sons to breathe the air of heaven.
E'en greed of gold—whose avaricious clutch
For six days past has beggar'd helpless babes,

Extorted tears from homeless widows' eyes,
And fill'd its coffers with ungodly gain,
In headlong haste to rival Mammon's fame—
Must halt for once, and cloak his canc'rous lust,
Or meet the blasting glance of public scorn.

All, all is calm. A bless'd armistice reigns—
And angel voices seem to whisper peace.

* * * * * *

All over Christendom's extended plains
Bright smiling groups of joyous youth appear,
Treading, with book in hand and agile step,
The honor'd pathway to the house of God.
Anon, a gentle hum pervades the aisles,
And softly floats along the ambient air,
As lisping tongues rehearse the storied scenes
Of oriental archives, penn'd by Heaven,
To guide th' expectant nations to the Cross.
Their ringing sounds, like chimes of silver bells—
Subdu'd by graver notes of riper age—
Roll through the groin'd and fretted vaults, to win
Symphonious voices from the echoing walls.
Seraphic sounds! 'Tis Zion's infant hosts
Before their King, in reverential mood,
In holy training for the wars of Heaven.

That modest, meek-eyed youth, of sylph-like form,
Unconscious of his worth, is gathering strength—
Immortal strength, of more than earthly mold—
To join the sacramental host elect,
And wield, in future times, an earthquake's pow'r
Against the lofty battlements of sin.

Yon cherub sister—lovely, young and fair;
Whose clust'ring locks her polish'd temples shade,
But leave in open view an angel smile,
T' expand the roses on her crimson cheek;
Her guileless bosom full of saintly zeal,
Her parting lips to soft inquiry fram'd;
Whose sparkling eyes with anxious gaze surveys
Each line that marks her teacher's speaking face,
While, bright with joy, she quaffs the heav'nly
    draught
That flows in luscious stream from lips she loves,
Surpassing far the nectar of the gods—
In years to come, with matron pride, shall nurse
Some infant Washington, whose lofty soul
In conscious majesty shall one day rise
To wrench the scepter from a tyrant's grasp,
And win the homage of a nation's heart;
Or train around the lov'd maternal knee

Some gifted Wesley, born to deathless fame,
And " pregnant with celestial fire," design'd
To re-illume the darksome temple-courts,
And kindle off'rings at ten thousand shrines.

Another, and another, bath'd in living light
At these pure founts, in coming years shall sweep
In ample orbit through the moral heavens,
And blend their radiance in the glowing skies.
* * * * * *
But richer splendor crowns the reigning day,
And clothes a hemisphere in rainbow dyes.

Hark! hark! The sweetly solemn bell
In measur'd tones now strikes the stilly air;
And chiming long and loud with sister sounds,
Now woos the stirring thousands from their homes,
To crowd the temple-gates, and think on heaven,
Where God's own altar burns, and purer light,
Celestial, streams from Zion's holy hill.

Transporting sight! Whole floods of human forms,
In cities-full, roll down the sounding streets.
The country's throng'd with well-attir'd groups,
Moving in silence to the house of prayer.

The solemn audience waits in mute suspense,
Till, rising to his consecrated desk,
The man of God appears. Th' Eternal Word
Inspires his glowing heart, and pours its truth
In healing volumes from his chasten'd lips;
Then bow'd in suppliant mood, his soul on fire,
He wings the faith of hundreds for the throne
Where boundless Mercy waits to lavish peace.
In earnest, calm appeal, his work begins.

His field embraces oriental climes,
Where human Hope was shorn of all her wealth,
And outrag'd Virtue sought her native skies.
His theme is high as heav'n and deep as hell;
But, ranging through its vast domains, he dwells
On " man's first disobedience and the fruit
Of that forbidden tree, whose mortal taste
Brought death into the world, with all our woe."
In burning words he paints the wrath pluck'd down,
To blast the Eden where the deed was done,
And brand with infamy the human race;
Then turns to Calvary with palms outspread,
And, full of faith and of the Holy Ghost,
Invokes th' incarnate God, once bath'd in blood,
Whose agonies upheav'd the startled globe

Till rocks were rent and graves disgorg'd their dead;
While weeping Nature, bending o'er His cross,
Her laws forgot, and shudder'd to the stars;
And sympathizing Mercy deign'd to drape
The sunless heavens with the pall of death.

Then, rapt in bliss, th' exulting preacher cries:
"The plea is heard! The Conq'ror claims His crown,
And Death and Hell lie crush'd beneath His feet!
Creation smiles, and angel guards descend;
A cloudy throne receives the rising Lord;
Unnumber'd seraphs crowd the gates of heaven,
To greet their conq'ring King with choral strains,
And Truth and Mercy kiss in long embrace."

The spell-bound audience feel th' unearthly theme,
And deep emotion starts the rising tear.
The reckless renegade no longer taunts,
Nor dares to spurn the Saviour from his soul.
Old age and youth in blending pathos melt,
And saints, enraptur'd, hail their coming heaven.

Oh hallow'd day! The sooth'd and soften'd crowd
In pensive rev'rence seek their sev'ral homes,

To stay themselves on God, and nobly foil
The fierce temptations of the opening week.

But still enlarge the scene. Far, far away,
Amid the blue Pacific's watery wastes,
Within the fiery Tropic's dazzling zone,
Owhyhee lifts above th' unfathom'd floods
His Alpine brow, to brave the heats of heaven
And vaunt his sparkling diadem of snow,
Where Mauna Roa's yawning crater spouts,
With thund'ring sounds, its cataracts of fire.
'Mid these inhospitable skies he bares
His rocky breast to break the ocean wave
Where kindred islands slumber on the deep,
And templed barbarism, steep'd in blood,
Late held its orgies on the smoking soil.

But Truth Eternal, borne upon the winds,
On high commission to the pagan world,
Its beacon-lights has shed through fog and gloom,
To rouse the torpid sleepers from their dreams,
And turn their guilty thousands to the Cross.

What wondrous prodigy is here! A birth—
A NATION'S MORAL BIRTH—*in one short day!*

Idolatry abjur'd, and sinless blood
From infants' veins no more to curse the land.
Oh blissful change! The sacred Sabbath now
With halcyon beams illumes the sea-bound group.

No steeple-bell disturbs the native wilds.
The forest sleeps, and lounging herds traverse
The sunlit plains, while Industry's at rest.
The bark canoe no longer skims the waves,
But, tether'd to the shore, with easy swing
It rocks responsive to the rippling tide.
The meshy net no finny game entoils,
But hangs on neighb'ring rocks, to drip and dry.
Nay, dreamy silence woos the beasts to roam
Without the dread of spear or whizzing shaft.
The timid kangaroo, from shady copse,
With nursling brood embowel'd in her folds,
Leaps free and far, to browse amid the cliffs.
The parakeet and tufted cockatoo
Their gaudy plumage flaunt in open air,
And chatter to the viewless winds unharm'd,
For now the tawny island hordes are still;
The palm-leaf chapel holds their manly forms,
As, bow'd in solemn mood, with hands outspread,
They join the fervent, soul-absorbing prayer

The Missionary sends to list'ning Heaven;
For savage nature—tam'd, and sooth'd, and sav'd—
Glad hails the hour, and, rising at its close,
Loud shouts redemption to the sounding seas.

   Heaven-consecrated day! The Godhead's boon!
The pledge hebdomadal of bliss to come!
O'er suppliant tribes and yielding kingdoms rule,
Till Hottentot and Hindoo, Turk and Moor,
And all the hosts of idol-serving knee,
Shall hail thy gladsome hours, and weekly swell
The world-wide anthem to the Christian's God!

   Then let the seasons roll, and Sabbaths come,
In pregustation of *eternal* rest!

   Soon, soon th' Apocalyptic trump shall ring
The herald thunders of the coming throne;
And buried millions leap from sod and sea,
To swell the pageant, and to meet their God.
The scene shall pass in quick but dread review.
The earth in seething flames—its millions doom'd—
And then the stormy elements shall sink,
Like fretful babes, to silence and to peace.

Great God, how grand! Th' ecstatic vision's true!
Th' ETERNAL SABBATH sheds its morning light,
Undimm'd by shadows and unspent by years;
While glory, streaming from Jehovah's eye,
Floods heaven with boundless bliss, and wakes
The hallelujahs of a WORLD REDEEM'D!

The Frown of God.

I HAVE seen the lightning's thong
   Fiercely lash the howling skies;
Heard the thunder's battle-gong
   Bid the giant tempest rise:

I have seen the midnight air
   Redden with the meteor's blaze;
Show'rs of sky-built rockets glare
   O'er a world's affrighted gaze:

I have heard the quaking ground
   Bellow to the whirlwind's blast;
Trembled at the startling sound,
   As the wild tornado pass'd:

I have felt creation rock
   To the earthquake's fearful tread;
While amid th' astounding shock
   Houseless thousands fear'd and fled:

I have groan'd with earthly woes—
   Battled with Misfortune's blast—

Gaz'd upon her dying throes,
   When a *mother* breath'd her last:

Yet amid these scenes of dread,
   Faith may spread her cloudless skies;
Man survive when Nature's dead,
   And in richer glory rise.

But *one horror*, deadlier far,
   Wraps the soul in Stygian gloom—
Leaves the world without a star,
   Pours its curse beyond the tomb.

Thunders, whirlwinds, earthquakes, raise
   Scarce a murmur on his ears,
When its piercing, with'ring blaze,
   Stirs the godless sinner's fears.

Let me meet the lightning's flash—
   Wear the thunder-scars of heav'n—
Reel amid the tempest's crash—
   Ride the floods, by cyclones driv'n:

Nor the drunken globe stand still—
   Earthquakes cleaving ev'ry sod;
Only shield me from *one ill!*—
   Save me from THE FROWN OF GOD!

Atlanta Crushed and Crowned.

A POEM

ADDRESSED TO THE GRADUATING CLASS OF THE ATLANTA MEDICAL COLLEGE, AND TO A LARGE AND ATTENTIVE AUDIENCE OF CITIZENS, ASSEMBLED IN THE CITY HALL, AUGUST 31ST, 1866.

[This young and flourishing city, which then contained about 18,000 inhabitants, was burnt, ravaged, and razed to its foundations, in the month of September, 1864, by the Federal forces under the command of Gen. Sherman, during the four years' merciless internecine war between the North and the South. But no sooner had peace been declared, than her returning thousands who had fled from their blazing homes, commenced to rebuild the ruined city and repair their wasted fortunes. Such an outlay of human energy has perhaps never been witnessed upon either continent, in the same length of time, and with no larger resources at command.]

On this bright gala-day busy memory sweeps,
   Upon broad, dusky wing, the exuberant past;
Numbers twenty-three months, and looks down on
      the heaps
   Of a war-ravag'd city, just breathing her last.

O God! what a vision glares red on the eye,
　　As earth-rocking thunders roll death through the streets,
And millions of capital melt in the sky,
　　As flames lash her buildings in wild, livid sheets!

Pandemonium shouts though her sulphurous hall
　　Till the revel infernal re-echoes through hell,
And the great master spirit responds to the call
　　That invokes his black curse over mountain and dell.

But enough!—there's a chapter of carnage and blood
　　That shall glow in red letters on history's page,
And shall rival the records of fire and of flood
　　That have scandal'd a Nero's and Attila's age.

　　*　　*　　*　　*　　*　　*

The demon of war had scarce quitted his prey,
　　And a conquering army its plunder and lust;
Its cataract roar had but just died away
　　Over bomb-shatter'd buildings, now crumbled to dust,

When thousands who fled from their blazing abodes,
　　To seek among strangers a covert from war,

Look'd longingly back o'er the blood-clotted roads,
   And their courage replum'd, under Hope's guiding star.

From the north, south, and east, the worn refugees come,
   And the west pours her quota in dust-cover'd throngs;
Each weeps o'er the wreck of his once happy home,
   And appeals to high Heav'n to avenge all his wrongs.

Full-soul'd and harmonious, they rush to new toils,
   And tax earth and air, sea and sky, for supplies;
And though myrmidon legions had gorg'd on her spoils,
   They swear by their manhood *"Atlanta shall rise!"*

'Twas a struggle of giants that knew no recoil!
   From morning till midnight resounded their blows;
The ingath'ring thousands no dangers could foil,
   Till the white flag of triumph in glory arose.

Old Balbec and Luxor for ages have slept,
   Redeemless and time-worn and shrouded in gloom;

O'er their huge broken columns the serpent has
    crept,
  And the yells of the jackal have sounded their doom.

But the deathless Gate City, though crush'd by the
    tread
  Of militant millions and thundering trains,
Has rent her own winding-sheet, burst from the dead,
  And the new pulse of life gushes warm through
    her veins!

Hail! hail! ye proud piles of undying renown!
  Your numbers shall swell as the ages roll on;
And your sun-lighted summits in grandeur look
    down
  On the contrite admirers your fame shall have won.

Fair Queen of the Midlands! thy reign shall extend
  From mountain to seaboard where commerce is
    found;
And Religion and Science in harmony blend,
  To foster the virtues their bulwarks surround.

Thus, lighting the landscape and blessing the land,
  The next generation thy name shall inspire,

To shout on the soil where thy monuments stand,
"*The souls of our fathers were proof against fire!*"

Ye parchmented heirs of Hippocrates, rouse!
　Your knowledge must quacks and impostors confound;
Your fond "Alma Mater" has laurel'd your brows,
　And Atlanta shall honor the sons she has crown'd.

She has own'd your profession, its temple repair'd,
　Dismantled and torn by the storm that has pass'd;
Then build up her fame with a labor unspar'd,
　That her gloom may be turn'd into glory at last.

"All Shall Be Well."

Dark, dark is the night, and the fierce winds are howling,
    And red, stunning thunderbolts leap from the sky;
The ocean is boiling! the heavens are scowling!
    And Nature weeps crystalline tears from on high.
        But wait, only wait, and the future shall tell,
        That God rules the *tempest*, and *all shall be well*.

The morning is coming! The storm-god is flying,
    And leaves in his rear all the spoils he has won;
Aurora is smiling; her chariot is nighing,
    And soft, golden cloudlets now herald the sun.
        Then wait, only wait, and the future shall tell,
        That God rules the *sunbeams*, and *all shall be well*.

    *   *   *   *   *   *

But again heaven darkens! The rain-floods are pouring,
    And torrents careering, roll wasting and wide.

The meadows are delug'd; the rivers are roaring,
   And flocks, herds and homes are entomb'd in the tide.
     But wait, only wait, and the future shall tell,
    That God rules the *deluge,* and *all shall be well.*

The wild inundation has calmly subsided—
   The streams to their channels submissive recoil;
A fertile alluvium thus is provided,
   And husbandmen reap richer fruits from the soil.
     Then wait, only wait, and the future shall tell,
    That God rules the *harvest,* and *all shall be well.*

    *   *   *   *   *   *

The cholera rages! An infant is sleeping—
   A gay, godless mother has rocked it to rest;
But Heaven claims the cherub!—the mother is weeping,
   And bows to her God with a spirit unblest.
     Still wait, only wait, and the future shall tell,
    That God rules in *sorrow,* and *all shall be well.*

That chamber is hallow'd, with angels attending
   Where childhood was budding, to bloom in the skies;

That mother has yielded—her pray'rs are ascending—
   Resign'd and submissive, peace beams from her eyes.
    Then wait, only wait, and the future shall tell,
    That God rules in *mercy,* and *all shall be well.*

Thus providence rules o'er the works of creation,
   And turns all the darkness of earth into light;
From sorrow educes the hopes of salvation,
   And crowns with its blessings misfortune and blight.
    Then wait, only wait, and the future shall tell,
    That GOD RULES FOREVER! and ALL SHALL BE WELL.

3*

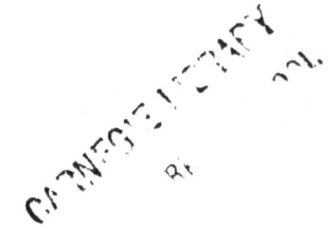

The War,

AND ONE OF ITS NOBLE VICTIMS.

A Tribute to the memory of THOMAS PRESTON SAMFORD, *First Lieutenant of Company M, First Texas Regiment, and youngest son of the Rev. Thomas Samford, formerly of Georgia, and a member of the Annual Conference of the Methodist Episcopal Church in that State, but since, a resident of Marshall, Harrison County, Texas, and now* NO MORE.

This noble young man and Christian hero, under the overpowering sense of the terrible emergency which periled the future destiny of the land that gave him birth, early threw himself into the front ranks of resistance to what he regarded unwarrantable encroachments of power; fought over the gory field, and through the smoke and carnage of Manassas, stood firm and unflinching in all the fights around Richmond, and was reserved for a patriot's grave and a hero's crown, on the distant soil of Maryland. Amid the roar of artillery and the clash of arms in the fearful struggle at Sharpsburg, while rushing on with a sword in one hand and a pistol in the other, in front of his faithful command, and crying out, with flushed cheek and flashing eye, " Strike, my boys, for your homes and your Confederacy !" he gloriously fell, a martyr to the cause of the South. Uncoffined and unknelled, he was quietly laid away in a soldier's "red winding-sheet," to await the rewards of the true and the brave.   A. M.

The earth has grown gray amid carnage and blood,
   And battle-fields reek with the gore of the slain;
The triumphs of pestilence, famine and flood,
   All pale in the glare of the war-god's reign.

But red though his scepter and stormy his sway
   Over antediluvian sons of the soil,
Surviving the Deluge, he widen'd his way
   To crush bleeding nations, or make them his spoil.

But what are the trophies of ages gone by—
   The laurels that cincture his storm-furrow'd brow?
Mere baubles of childhood, that fade in his eye,
   To glories that crown him a conqueror now.

A continent shakes to the weight of his wheel,
   And panoplied millions collide on the plain;
The mountains re-echo the clangor of steel,
   And rivers run red with the blood of the slain!

Here Mind, like the maniac, sunders her chains,
   And bounds to the touch that has open'd her cell;
In perilous flight, circles Nature's domains,
   And peers to the heights where the cherubim dwell,

Creation, conceding her power to explore,
    Unbosoms her secrets for ages conceal'd;
And Science, from deeps never sounded before,
    Uncaverns her stores for the camp and the field.

The earth, air and ocean, are summon'd at last
    To swell the key-note of the warrior's fame;
The hills, disembowel'd, give ore for the blast,
    And dragon-like monsters emerge from the flame.

The mountains are tunnel'd with powder and pick,
    For subterrene armies and thundering trains;
And herald dispatches fly vivid and thick,
    Outsweeping the winds when the hurricane reigns.

While out on the deep a whole argosy rides
    Of huge "pachydermata," scaly with steel,
Spurning bullets and bombs from their war-beaten sides,
    As the charger the gadfly that lights on his heel.

Far down in the floods where the sea-monsters play,
    A sulphurous earthquake in embryo lies,
Till transport or monitor steers in its way,
    And a submarine shock turns its keel to the skies.

The seacoast and cities with gun-metal groan,
    And stunning explosions roll back from the shore;
While the "thunderer" Jove is outvoic'd on his throne,
    As the bumble-bee's hum by Niagara's roar.

Such, such, in this iron-cast age, is the sight,
    When philosophy wings ev'ry fury with flame,
To decimate nations—to blast and to blight,
    And blazon with blood-stains the conqueror's name.

O God! what an age! Let posterity tell
    To late generations the wars of their sires,
When Pluto's abhorr'd mythological hell
    Was mild, to the blaze of their battle-field fires.

Yet "offences will come," for the gateway is wide
    Whose portals are throng'd with the selfish and vile,
That gracelessly pander to passion and pride,
    And gloat o'er the ruin of the land they defile.

But justice eternal still poises the scales,
    Though rock'd by ambition or freighted with gold;
And, thron'd in her temple, her verdict prevails
    To smite the despoiler with curses untold.

The demagogue brawls—supple minions encore,
  And cudgels rebound from undignified heads;
The masses are madden'd from mountain to shore,
  And the cordage of government's torn into shreds.

Spurning counsels and cautions—blind, reckless, and bold—
  Fanatical zealots lash on the affray;
And case-harden'd Shylocks turn blood into gold,
  While God's holy altars are ravag'd for prey.

Thus fiercely and far the red crusade prevails,
  For crush'd constitutions and laws rule no more;
'Mid the outcries of orphans and lone widows' wails,
  A hungry menagerie riots in gore.

War! war! from the thunders that peal at her gates;
  Lifts high her portcullis and pours out her hosts;
Far North and far South, through a cordon of States,
  The human tornado fills Hades with ghosts.

Hark! hark! 'tis our bugle that sounds to the field,
  And our yeomanry's shouts rend the air as they go.
On! onward they rush, without helmet or shield—
  A torrent of heroes, to bear down the foe.

The wild roll of battle now echoes afar,
　　And marshal'd battalions move on to the fray;
Unleash'd from their collars, the bloodhounds of war
　　Yelp shrill to the winds, as they haste to their prey.

As links of wrought steel they are leagued against
　　　　pow'r,
　　And strike for their altars, their homes, and their
　　　　lives;
The storm-cloud has burst, and its masses still low'r,
　　Yet high floats their flag where the fierce tempest
　　　　drives.

Bold columns through deep mountain gorges are fil'd,
　　To pour like an avalanche down on the plain,
Where blood-sheeted foes are in pyramids pil'd,
　　And the vulture and eagle are gorg'd on the slain.

Thus rolling in storm over forest and flood,
　　The gods might have envied the chariot of Mars;
As massacred legions are bathing in blood,
　　And a war-ravag'd empire smokes to the stars.

The Genius of History, pois'd o'er the land
　　Where high Southern *honor* defies Northern *steel*,

Selects from our heroes the morally grand,
    To fix on their brows immortality's seal.

'Mid the ranks of young Hectors thus wedded to fame,
    Whose names are enstarr'd on our temple's proud dome—
One beautiful orb its position shall claim
    For ages, to light up the patriot's home.

He was born for his country, and, plum'd cap and heel,
    Was rock'd by the storms of a Texian sky;
His fiery Caduceus well temper'd steel
    Flashed quick as the lightning when foes caught his eye.

A patriot father, now hoary with years,
    Had lean'd on his "Joseph," and liv'd in his child;
The patriarch struggled—he conquer'd in tears—
    Then gave him to God and his country, and smil'd.

Thus he mov'd to the field with a grandeur of soul
    That startled the coward and cheer'd on the brave;

No bribe in his palm and no wine in his bowl—
    His shield was his *conscience;* his guerdon, a *grave.*

He stood in the ranks an Achilles in form—
    Elastic and muscular, graceful and large;
A model of manhood in calm or in storm,
    To shine in the Senate or tow'r in the charge.

The throb of *his* heart was the pulse of his men—
    The flash of his eye was their beacon in fight;
He dash'd over hilltop or bounded through fen
    With the plunge of the lion when lambs are in sight.

At Manassas he breasted the first shock of war,
    Enroll'd in the " Stonewall" immortal brigade;
He flam'd through its carnage, led on by his star,
    And sought new arenas to flesh his young blade.

That star hung in crimson, portentous and pale,
    O'er the far field of Sharpsburg, the soil of the foe;
As the war-cry of squadrons rang loud on the gale,
    And troops roll'd in columns to work deeds of woe.

In stern, gloomy grandeur our columns stood still,
    Like Ætna's proud cone when his thunders are near;

Until long-restrained Vengeance had master'd their will,
    And burst through its barriers, in quenchless career.

From heart-throbbing thousands, equipt and align'd,
    A hail-storm of iron in fury was hurl'd,
As if thunder, volcano and earthquake combin'd
    To sink a doom'd nation and startle the world.

'Twas a struggle of giants that sham'd Homer's gods,
    Who flung rifted rocks from the mountain's torn side;
Their missiles of vengeance but green trunks and sods —
    Mythological pomp, with demoniac pride.

But the brow of our hero loom'd lofty and grand,
    Like Olympus when shaking the storm from his side,
As, with saber uprais'd in the grasp of his hand,
    And pistol unbelted, whole ranks he defied.

With a shout on his lip and a blow on his blade,
    He strode over ranks of the dying and dead;

His phalanx respond, as they rush to his aid,
   But alas! *the pale star from its heavens had fled!*

He fell! But a demon unchamber'd that ball
   That rifled the heart's-blood of virtue and truth—
That blighted the homestead and darken'd the hall
   Where age had long bask'd in the smiles of his youth.

But, peaceful and pure, and in sight of his rest,
   His soul on the wing for its crown in the sky;
With *woman* to weep o'er the warrior's breast,
   It was honor and triumph and *glory*, TO DIE!

No hearse wav'd its ebony plumes o'er the dead;
   No pompous procession encircled his grave;
Unknell'd and uncoffin'd, he pillow'd his head
   On the soil of the stranger — a friend to the brave.

O God! shall despoilers still ravage the land,
   Unglutted with slaughter, unsated with blood?
Sure virtue *must* triumph, and judgment demand
   The dark day of vengeance — the doomsday of God!

Salvation may linger, and scourge follow scourge,
  Till Moloch and Mammon lie prostrate and crush'd,
But the *nation* from gloom *shall to glory emerge,*
  And her wild wail of horror forever be hush'd.

Then sleep, noble son of a God-trusting sire!
  Unstirr'd by the tread of huge caisson or gun;
Sleep! sleep with thy compeers that waded through blood,
  Till wak'd to the fame which thy virtues have won.

Thy country's now tipped with the light of the morn,
  And the nations but wait for the full flood of day;
Thy name shall then reach generations unborn,
  When T. PRESTON SAMFORD has molder'd to clay.

Supplement to "The War."

Addressed by the author to his long esteemed friend WILLIAM F. SAMFORD, A.M., LL.D., *of Auburn, Alabama — brother of the sainted Preston.*

But still I would linger to hear from the past
    The echoes which Memory rings on my ears;
The thoughts which they stir for a life-time shall last,
    When the heart-stricken household has outliv'd its tears.

One son of the group in that ancestral home,
    The wing'd god of eloquence richly endow'd;
His tongue like the lightning that plays round the dome,
    And heralds the thunder that rolls from the cloud.

In life's blushing morning he sat at my board,
    Confiding and truthful and brilliant and strong;
Fresh plum'd, like the eaglet, he sported and soar'd,
    And gaz'd on creation, in rapture and song.

There patron and protégé knelt at one shrine,
    And heart beat to heart with the pendulum's truth;
That virgin affection shall never decline,
    But live as the loves of Naomi and Ruth.

His heaven-born virtues spurn'd pagod and pelf,
    And honor unshorn rul'd his generous breast;
His noble young heart sought a duplicate self:
    He woo'd and he won, and the union was blest.

A pure, lovely matron now sits by his side,
    The queen of his household and light of his life;
The *mother* more dear than the beautiful bride —
    For grief finds a balm in the smiles of a wife.

Three decades of years with their deeds have gone by,
    And millions have sunk as the rain-drops at sea;
The sage and the stripling in common dust lie,
    But "William" and friendship survive yet for me.

Nay, *friendship's* too formal and soulless a name
    For the deeper and richer and holier grace
That burns for an age with unquenchable flame
    In souls that unite in angelic embrace.

Oh! give me the glory of midsummer morn,
   Suffusing the hilltops and warming the vale;
And leave to the bats and the owlets forlorn,
   The moon-lighted landscape, so *cold* and so *pale*.

The loves of the angels are kindled and ton'd
   In the glow of the Godhead that beams from their eyes,
Where day without night is in splendor enthron'd,
   To burn on forever in rose-tinted skies.

The Train.

RESPECTFULLY DEDICATED, BY THE AUTHOR, TO THAT IMPORTANT AND USEFUL CLASS OF MEN, RAILROAD CONDUCTORS.

WHEN bards long ago sang the ocean,
   And mountain and river and plain,
They felt not the thrilling emotion
   Inspired by the thundering train.

They ne'er heard the sound of the *whistle*,
   And steam never entered their brain;
They lauded the "rose" and the "thistle,"
   But *never* the thundering train.

We propose, then, in grateful ovation,
   An humble, pretensionless strain;
And, enthus'd by our novel vocation,
   Chant praise to the thundering train.

   *   *   *   *   *

The CONDUCTOR leads on the procession—
   The lord of his special domain;

No claimant disputes his possession—
　He *reigns* on the thundering train.

Neither pageants nor levees delay him;
　No claims are allowed to detain;
The prince and the pauper obey him,
　While ruling his thundering train.

Though the fields and the crops are in danger
　From drought, or from down-pouring rain,
To both in his sphere he's a stranger,
　Exempt, on his thundering train.

Let the soldier abandon his cottage,
　And wade through the bloody campaign—
His fare only hoe-cake or pottage;
　He *feasts* on his thundering train.

While thousands in cities are dying,
　And armies are counting their slain,
With free ventilation he's flying,
　Unharm'd, on his thundering train.

No Blackstone engrosses his vision—
　No ledger his eyesight to strain;

He guards against breaks and collision,
    And smiles on his thundering train.

The triumphs that crown his dominions,
    The nabob and churl may disdain;
But, heedless of captious opinions,
    He's king on the thundering train.

He rolls over valleys and fountains,
    And skims o'er the emerald plain,
Or sweeps through the gorges of mountains,
    O'erhanging his thundering train.

His engineer, true to his station,
    Stands fronting the tempest and rain,
To guide to their safe destination
    The crowds on the thundering train.

Would the Cyclops he bridles rush faster?
    He blusters and hisses in vain;
For he's grasp'd by the hand of a *master!*
    And smooth rolls the thundering train.

He stops not when sunlight is closing,
    And Venus is scepter'd to reign;

But startles the dull and the dozing
    By the roar of his thundering train.

His head-lights are ever kept burning—
    His rear-beacon shines not in vain;
The *first* floods the track at each turning,
    The *last* guards the thundering train.

Orion, the heavens adorning,
    Looks down on the glimmering plain,
And a glance from the Star of the Morning
    Illumines his thundering train.

He scatters the wonders of science,
    To national commerce germane;
And to lightning and storm bids defiance—
    All safe on his thundering train.

His presence enlivens each nation,
    Enlighten'd, devout, or profane;
While multitudes crowd ev'ry station,
    To welcome his thundering train.

He carries the Cross and its story
    To heathen beyond the deep main;

And heralds its forthcoming glory,
   On board of his thundering train.

Thus kingdoms and peoples, united
   By brotherhood's magical chain,
Whose lands the Conductor has lighted,
   Shall shout to the thundering train.

When the nations, in harmony blended,
   Shall hail the millennial reign,
And Messiah to earth has descended—
   Farewell to the THUNDERING TRAIN!

The Triumph of Joseph,

BEFORE THE COURT OF THE EGYPTIAN KING.

Purity Rewarded.

Yon chariot is rolling in state!
  Young Joseph, the friend of the king,
Sits vestur'd in robes of the great—
  On his finger the royal gold ring.

O'er his virtuous bosom descends
  A circle of Ophir's pure ore;
While the shout of the criers ascends,
  And thousands are bowing before.

King Phar'oh thus honors the youth
  Whose purity shone as the sun;
Whose modesty, wisdom and truth,
  The monarch's high confidence won.

All Egypt exults in his reign,
  While famine and pestilence fly;
And her storehouses, groaning with grain,
  Yield Canaan itself a supply.

The Mount of Holiness.

How proudly the peak of yon mountain
   Looks down from the arch of the sky,
As in grandeur it shadows the fountain
   That sports through its cliffs upon high!

The soft silver light of the morning
   Encircles its emerald brow,
Ere the peasant by chanticleer's warning
   Is roused, at its base, to the plow.

It stands in its lofty seclusion,
   Where sunshine and peace ever reign;
Far, far from the gloom and confusion,
   That checker the populous plain.

As the lion the dew from his shoulder,
   It shakes the wild storm from its side;
While below, where the torrent grows bolder,
   Whole flocks are entomb'd in the tide.

Thus thron'd on the heights of devotion—
    Sublime in their hallowing glow—
The Christian transcends the commotion
    That rocks the whole region below.

When Sorrow her storm-cloud has driv'n,
    And deep moral darkness abounds,
He bathes in the sunlight of Heav'n,
    And smiles on the gloom that surrounds.

Absorb'd in the rapturous vision
    That catches his heavenward eye,
He heeds not the whirl and collision
    Of crowds that are hurrying by.

Secure in his bright elevation,
    He feels, but as mist from the cloud,
The sweep of that vast inundation
    That whelms the licentious crowd.

Thence, thence let me meet the Eternal,
    And reign above fire and flood!
Encinctur'd with beauties supernal,
    And crown'd with the glory of God.

A Reminiscence.

(FOR HIS WIFE.)

Written by the author when far from home, on Valentine's Day, February 14, 1851.

DEAR wife of my bosom! when, youthful and gay,
We met on the eve of our bright wedding day,
In the blush of young beauty you stood by my side,
And my heart hail'd with rapture its lovely young bride.

But twenty-four summers have since roll'd away,
And the glossy brown locks have been soften'd to gray;
A staid, cheerful *mother* now sits by my side —
The *matron* more lov'd than the *beautiful bride*.

The Balloon's Ascension.

The plain of the grand Champs de Mars is alive,
   And Paris her thousands pours out to the sight,
As bees rush in columns, deserting their hives,
   And cluster in swarms round the queen in her flight.

A mammoth balloon hangs suspended in air,
   Collaps'd, uninflated, and cabled to earth;
The gas-tubes disgorge—human multitudes stare—
   And the first inspiration proclaims a *new birth*.

The beautiful globe, as it breathes, swells apace,
   Enlarges, and rises till rotund in form;
Then struggles to sever the cords at its base,
   To bathe in the sunlight above cloud and storm.

But, bound and engirdled, its essays are vain,
   Till the master balloonist has sever'd its ties;
Then, loos'd from its moorings, it mounts from the plain,
   And buoyant and towering steers for the skies.

Thus, grand though its outline, the Soul lingers here,
    Contracted and crush'd in Satanic embrace;
Nor claims its Elysium, nor soars to its sphere,
    Till expanded and volum'd and buoyant by grace.

Then, spurning its captor, but biding its time,
    It swells toward heaven, impatient to rise,
Till the blow of release from the Master Sublime
    Unprisons the captive with gladd'ning surprise.

Then, free as the air, to the regions of light,
    Elastic and soaring, it leaves the world's gaze;
No sweep of the telescope follows its flight,
    Engirt by the Godhead and lost in its blaze.

The Noachian Deluge.

In yon blue deep where float, in boundlessness
Remote, the millionary orbs of heaven—
Grand epochs, congruous with th' eternal plans—
In long, long cycles of returning years
Attend the presence of the reigning God.

Revolving centuries chime their grand events
Throughout the mighty frame-work of the skies,
Where solar centers move their trains of worlds,
And suns and satellites in dazzling pomp
Their gorgeous systems wheel through space profound;
Creation's glowing frontier coasting far,
And blending revolutions vast, sublime,
In starry poise upon one awful point!
That point, the glory of the Milky Zone—
Great Maëdler's focal universe*—perhaps

---

* The distinguished German astronomer, Maëdler, has, by a long and laborious course of investigation, discovered—as he believes—what we have long regarded as existing somewhere in space, viz., the stupendous stationary central system, about which all the solar systems in the stellar universe are supposed to revolve, in long cycles of centuries.

The council-chamber of the King of kings,
Shekinah's lofty antitype, where God
Is seen, amid the cherubim enthroned,
And Nature's starlit temple spreads its dome,
To gather incense from ten thousand shrines.

O fathomless abyss of wonders new!
Where thought adventurous reels, and shuns the gaze,
Shrinks back to earth, and on her planet-home
Finds more than scope to try her loftiest pow'rs.
And yet that home, among the works of God
How small! A ray—a pale, a lonely ray—
Amid th' effulgence of the blazing skies!
Still, still this minim orb, by birthright ours,
To finite minds outspreads phenomena
Of startling grandeur—staggering hoary faith,
Confounding reason and o'erwhelming thought.

The EARTH then be our theme: one grand event
In all her time-worn history enough
To crowd the present hour.

      Age after age,
Her scath'd and rugged form had proudly borne
The dread catastrophes which rudely grav'd

Their petty triumphs on her marble hills;
But still she stood to bide her future woes.

Of changes wrought by deep convulsive throes
Wide propagated from her burning heart*—
Unbedding seas, upheaving continents,
Submerging mountain-chains in ocean deeps,
And cleaving chasms for her frighten'd floods †—
While, bursting from her swoll'n and ruptur'd veins
Three hundred rivers pour, of liquid fire,‡
To blight the land and waste the fuming seas.
Of these we nothing say: 'tis ours to mark
One scene—one dismal scene—where Vengeance rul'd,
And guilty millions met their changeless doom.

MAN—rebel man—had spurn'd the reign of Heaven,
And fiercely rush'd to scenes of lust and blood.

---

* The well sustained doctrine of the earth's interior or central heat is here recognized.

† These geological changes have actually taken place, and their consequent phenomena are plainly recorded among the mountain upheavals, disrupted strata, and fossil and mineral deposits of our globe.

‡ The largest estimated number of active volcanoes now upon the earth's surface.

A godless progeny, in lapse of years,
Wide spread the infecting curse, till, steep'd in sin,
The drunken nations toppled o'er the abyss
Which flaming Justice opened at their feet.
Retiring Mercy dropp'd the final tear,
And exiled Virtue sought her native skies.

  One aged sire, of all the abandon'd throng,
Still worshiped God, and kept His altars pure.
Six hundred years had wreathed his noble brow
With fleecy honors, and his faithful voice
For five score past had warn'd his wayward race.
The faithful few whose beacon lights had shone
In lonely luster 'mid the moral gloom
Were gone, and Vengeance hurried to her work.
Old Lamech clos'd his eyes in peace—and, *last*,
The hoary-hair'd Methuselah, worn down
With pious labors of a thousand years,
Was call'd to rest, to shun the gath'ring storm.
The stage was clear; then why should judgment
    sleep,
Perdition linger, or fierce wrath delay?
They did not sleep, nor linger, nor delay.
Earth, lab'ring to her trembling poles, seem'd task'd
To evolve the Almighty's desolating curse.

But let us rise to Contemplation's heights,
And gaze across the gulf of ages past,
To realize the horrors of the scene.

    *   *   *   *   *   *

Behold, how calm the earth! how still the seas!
Portentous silence reigns; while far and wide
The dreamy air seems bound in Lethean spell,
And nature's breathing hosts no change suspect.
'Tis morning's dewy hour. The god of day
On noiseless wheel mounts up the steep of heaven,
And sheds his purple beams o'er lake and hill.
Above, below, around, creation's hush'd,
As if in dread presentiment of doom.
A pause—an *awful pause!*—foretokens ruin.

But hark! A distant hum disturbs the air;
Earth's stirring thousands swell the echoing din,
Nor mark pale nature's signals in the skies,
Her deathlike stillness and her pulseless frame.
The thoughtless sons of fashion hurry by,
To feast and dance—alas! their final hour.
The worldly merchant lauds his wares, and boasts
The yearly gains his practic'd skill insures.
The plodding peasant goads his lazy team,
And counts his golden harvest in advance;

While bloated debauchees abhor the light,
And, lock'd in guilty arms, provoke their fate.

No eye is heavenward. Lust and Mammon rage,
And recking Passion, stooping o'er the mane,
With sounding lash and rowels dipp'd in blood,
Still plies his smoking steed and braves his doom;
While gory Murder—fiercest of his train—
Snuffs th' infected air, and madly waves
His crimson poniard as he posts to hell.
Oh! fearful prelude to the impending curse!
Dread spectacle! A WORLD WITHOUT A GOD!

But mark the darkening heavens, the fiery sun,
The rolling vapors, and the deep'ning storm!
Egyptian blackness shrouds the morning skies,
And raking whirlwinds run their wild career!
Red bolts leap thick from clouds surcharg'd with
    death!
Loud herald thunders ring the nations' knell,
And earth "gives signs of woe that all is lost."
The deaf'ning clarion of the world-wide storm
Awakes the angry deep. Then, palsy-struck,
The shudd'ring globe upon its axis halts;
And hoary ocean, restless in his bed,

Uplifts his giant form to Alpine height;
And, gathering mightier strength, from pole to pole
Rolls coastward all his world of waves, and swells
The wild uproar of struggling elements;
Then dashing on, with fearful shock assails
His granite barriers of two thousand years,
O'erplunges far their pigmy heights, and whelms
In wat'ry woe the founder'd continents.*

Old Etna groans, and hisses from his caves,
To spurn the intruding tides that climb his steeps
And dare his dismal flames. Wild waters plunge
In frightful fury down his furnace throat.
He heaves amain; his red foundations rock;

---

* Infidelity once carped about the impossibility of submerging the highest mountains with the amount of water contained in all the oceans and seas of our globe; and therefore affected to ridicule the Mosaic account of the Deluge. This point, however, has been long since settled, by calculations made upon safe data, in favor of the divine historian. The author has here conjectured, that as the fluids and solids of our globe, by uniform velocity of revolution, had acquired a common "motal inertia," it was only necessary for the Divine fiat to check for a moment the usual speed of its diurnal movement; and, as the waters were mobile, and could not immediately accommodate themselves to the sudden change of inertia in the solids, the inevitable result would be the outbreak of oceans, seas and lakes over their respective barriers, and the consequent submergence of continents: a physical result readily illustrated by the plunge of a fluid over the lip of a containing vessel which has been suddenly stopped when in the midst of a uniform and brisk motion.

And hot disgorging from his molten deeps
Whole cataracts of fire, he madly spouts
The boiling seas to drench th' astonish'd skies.
Vesuvius too makes battle with the deep,
And flood and fire contend for mastery.

Tomboro,* thund'ring till his roar is heard
Three hundred leagues, confronts the ocean-shock;
And, like a boa scotch'd and nursing wrath,
In forkéd fury shoots out tongues of fire.

Fierce Hecla frowns, and from his crater rolls
Portentous smoke in volumes through the air;
But feels his lurid throne profoundly quake,
As revolutionary waves—asleep
For twenty centuries at his rock-bound base—
O'erleap his bulwarks and ascend his heights.

---

*A volcanic mountain in Sumbawa, one of the islands of the Grecian Archipelago, from which one of the most fearful eruptions recorded in history took place, commencing on the 5th of April, 1815, and continuing until July following; the explosions being heard to the distance of 960 geographical miles in one direction and 720 in the opposite; overwhelming the island with blazing lava, volcanic tufa and ashes, leaving only 20 survivors out of a population of 12,000, and disgorging from its crater solid material enough to form a globe six miles in diameter.

Deep, sinuous mountain gorges madly foam
With pent-up seas, impatient of restraint,
And new-born gulfs are cradled in the clouds.
Sea-monsters, from their briny homes afar,
Float buoyant over Andes' proudest peaks,
And gambol in the floods 'twixt earth and heaven;
While currents sweep in vast gyrations round,
And furious maelstroms whirl with deaf'ning roar,
Till, loosened from their icy beds on high,
Huge avalanches, tumbling headlong down,
Are in the mighty vortices engorged.

O God of grandeur! who shall sketch the scene,
When outrag'd justice stirs th' Eternal arm
To signalize its pow'r in judgment pomp?

* * * * * *

Behold how wide stern desolation reigns!
Confounded crowds of staring skeptics fly
In dripping garments from the vengeful floods,
As, pouring fast, they rise to loftier heights.
Old age is there—grown lank and gray in sin—
But eschews still to die; and clamb'ring slow,
With crutch and crippled gait, seeks neighb'ring
    mounds,

In vain attempt to escape its stormy doom.
Soft infancy is there, and, rudely torn
In shiv'ring terror from the parent breast,
Sinks down asphyctic in the yawning seas.

  The deluge grows till mountains, undermin'd
And nodding to their heaving base, are seen
With thundering plunge engulf'd to rise *no more!*
Ten thousand whirlpools float their millions by,
  With arms outstretch'd for help. Their piercing
      shrieks
But swell the bellowings of the angry seas;
While cities, bowed beneath the briny scourge,
Disgorge their drowning throngs — then sink en-
    tomb'd.
Each lofty pinnacle that longest braves
The grand debacle in its upward swoop,
Hangs clustered thick with crowds of human forms,
Transfix'd with horror, as the lawless waves
In tow'ring vengeance lash their tottering feet.

  O God! the hour has come! One moment more,
And all is gone! The last lone cliff is reach'd—
A final breaker laves the screaming groups—

The monarch mountain of a thousand peaks
Succumbs! PROUD EVEREST* IS SEEN NO MORE!

 * * * * * *

Far eastward † rolls th' impetuous, stormy tide,
Till oceans, seas and lakes in solemn league
Their billows blend, and, compassing the zones,
With liquid winding-sheet invest the globe.
The EARTH is all a TOMB, and judgment's *sealed!*

 * * * * * *

But see! There floats upon the blue expanse,
In dubious shape, a dim and distant thing!
In passive mood it yields to warring waves,
Then mounts their crests, and hovers in the air.
It nears apace! and, hurried by the winds,
To bold dimensions grows! Now full reveal'd—

---

* Mount Everest, in the Himalaya range, is now regarded the loftiest mountain summit on the earth, being 29,002 feet (nearly 5½ miles) above the level of the sea.

† The revolution of the earth upon its axis being from west to east, a sudden suspension of its motion would precipitate the inundating waters over their respective boundaries in that direction, so that the western continent of North and South America would be first submerged by the waves of the Northern and Southern Pacific; Europe, Northern Asia, and Northern Africa, by the Northern Atlantic; Middle and Southern Asia by the Mediterranean, Red Sea, Sea of Arabia, and Bay of Bengal; and New Holland and the East India Islands by the Indian Ocean, &c.; interestingly corresponding—especially in the Northern Hemisphere, where most geological examinations have been made—to the line of direction along which the erratic rocks of Europe and the bowlders of the United States have been evidently borne by some great flood of waters from their original beds.

A massive pile—it moves in kingly state,
High booming o'er the fathomless abyss!

   Amid the opening sunshine, and the storm.
Now rolling back to leave the floods at rest,
A gorgeous rainbow spans its lofty brow,
Enthron'd in splendor on the bending skies!
On! onward still it drives o'er deeps profound—
O'er Alps' and Apennines' and Andes' peaks—
Nor stoops to own the grandeur of their rank.
A *patriarchal palace* stands confess'd—
The mammoth wonder of a world inhum'd—
Surcharg'd with life, to stock a world to come!

   Nor helm nor compass steers the steady prow.
Supernal Wisdom guides its bold career;
For Noah's household rides upon the seas,
Encircled by the promise of his God!

   Float on, immortal voyager! thy faith,
Fast anchor'd by the Eternal throne, controls
The Godhead's pledg'd and boundless pow'r; and when
The fissur'd earth shall swallow up her seas,
And liberated mountains peer again
Above the ransom'd plains, thou still shalt live,
The godly sire of millions yet unborn!

Sacred Localities in Palestine.

READ BEFORE THE OXFORD SUNDAY SCHOOL.

Ever hallow'd on earth are the spots that were trod
By the feet of Messiah, the crown'd Son of God.
As landmarks they stand on the highway of years,
To move passing millions to smiles and to tears.

Old Palestine, wasted, these trophies still boasts,
That shine on her hilltops and speak from her coasts.
No ruin can blast them, no power entomb;
Their beacons shall burn till the morning of doom.

The deeds of the past rise again to the eye,
As the grand panorama rolls silently by,
All radiant with scenes that enrapture the soul,
And shall light up the heav'ns when the last thunders roll.

* * * * * *

Mount Zion's hoar brow monumentally looms
Over decades of ages, and kingdoms and tombs

Once lustrous with glories by God's temple giv'n,
Now shorn of her splendors, but pointing to heaven.

Dear Olivet still courts the sun as he shines
O'er her green grassy slopes, and her figs and her vines;
Unchalleng'd she wears all her honors alone—
For a cloud from *her brow* bore the Lord to his throne.

Let us weep over Bethany—name ever sweet,
Euphonious and dear ! — in its lowly retreat;
For its glory is gone; not a vestige remains,
Save the halo which history sheds o'er its plains.

Blest Lake of the Hills, ever lov'd Galilee !
Thy shores and thy waters are dearest to me.
In childhood thy stories were grav'd on my heart
As intaglios on marble, enchisel'd by art.

For thy bright, limpid wavelets once nurs'd the Man-God,
And rock'd Him to rest on their soft swelling flood;
And when wild Euroclydon rush'd from his caves,
And lash'd into madness thy foam-crested waves,

At a word from His lips, and a glance from His eye,
Fled the dark howling tempest in silence to die;
And thy poor throbbing bosom pulsated no more,
But fondly embrac'd Him and bore Him to shore.

Little Bethlehem's heights rest in peace as of yore,
But her " star" and her " manger" are long since *no more.*
There the great Shepherd-King saw his first light of morn;
There his antitype, Christ, for the nations was born.

O'er her midnight an angelic anthem roll'd high,
And the song of salvation first rang through the sky.
In her bosom she cradled the world's infant Lord,
And sheltered His manhood, and bow'd and ador'd.

To the ear of the stranger no echo resounds;
Her streets lie neglected, and silence surrounds;
Still the Judean mountains o'erhang her west line,
And their steep, terrac'd sides nurse the olive and vine.

Though dismantled and peel'd, and inglorious *now*,
Immortality's seal has been fixed on her brow;

And she bides but her time, till her offspring again
Shall revisit His birthplace, in glory to reign.

When the "Red Cross" has conquer'd, and hell's in despair,
And the angel of doom sounds his blast on the air;
When the sleeping redeem'd shall the summons obey,
And shall muster by millions to hail the *Great Day*—

As the down-pouring legions of bliss greet the earth,
And Bethlehem points to her *manger* and *birth*,
Angelic hosannas shall roll o'er her plains,
And the broad empyrean resound with the strains.

But peace, joy and beauty are transient from birth,
For bliss must be follow'd by blight upon earth.
Dread contrast! when brightness and loveliness fly,
And yield up their reign, amid darkness to die.

Thus o'er the brook Kedron Gethsemane shone
When her garden embower'd her Lord all alone;
But estrang'd and forlorn, as she now strikes the sight,
She seems left to mourn o'er His *last dismal night*.

But peerless on earth is the last spot we name,
Where the focaliz'd vengeance of hell shot its flame;
Where darkness at noonday, and earthquake and blood,
Proclaim'd human bliss, and the reign of a God.

The fame of these triumphs old Calvary won,
And honor'd her God through His conquering Son;
While her Cross shall still live in the mem'ries of heaven,
And homage divine to its Victim be given.

Like sculptur'd mausolea rear'd in the East,
To hand down the fame of their heroes deceas'd,
These evergreen landmarks shall tow'r over tombs,
To eternize the scenes which the Cross still illumes.

The Song-Bird Uncaged.

How sweet are the notes which the song-bird sings,
   From his perch in his wire-bound cell!
How plaintive his strain through the parlor rings,
   Like the tones of a silver bell!

The sunshine streams through his lattic'd cage,
   And the wild winds fan his breast;
He longs for the mate of his fledgeling age,
   And carols himself to rest!

All is lonely and still as the night rolls by;
   And he hangs on the time-worn wall
Till the day-beams shoot from the morning sky
   And blaze through the old oak hall.

Through his homely wicket the day peers in,
   And reveals no barrier there;
For his keep—not closed by a bolt or pin—
   Stands wide to the balmy air.

Arous'd from his dreams with a scream and spring,
   He bursts from his long night's tomb;

With a hymn on his tongue and the dew on his wing,
    He escapes to his mountain home.

Thus away from the realms of perennial day,
    And the land of the pure and blest,
The soul looks out from its lodge of clay,
    And longs for its endless rest.

When its skies are aglow with the Godhead's rays,
    'Tis in vain that the chill wind blows;
It exults in the prospect of balmier days,
    And sinks into holy repose.

Now the night steals on—the relentless night
    Of the lonely and lifeless tomb—
Where a star burns not, nor a glow-worm's light
    Ever gleams on the dismal gloom.

But a *prince* sleeps there, and the death-king flies
    From the courts of his ghostly reign,
As the *last* sun purples the eastern skies,
    And the life-pulse bounds again.

A monarch springs from the conquer'd tomb,
    And ascends to his throne on high;
And as angel millions escort him home,
    Hallelujahs rend the sky.

ELEGY ON
Little Charles Meminger Capers.*

A Tribute of Affection from his Grandfather, the Author.

Our sweet little cherub, farewell! farewell!
   Thou hast fled in the morn of life;
Soon plum'd for heaven, and too bright to dwell
   In this world of sin and strife.

But sudden and loud as the thunder-shock
   To the sinking lamb in the fold,
While the helpless, frightened and flying flock
   Its motionless form behold,

Was the stunning call from the angel world,
   That sunder'd the ties of earth,
Which in *four short years* had their spirals curl'd
   Round the hearts that gave them birth.

But the deed is done, and our treasure's gone!
   'Twas a loan from heaven, at best;

---

*Accidentally shot, at four years of age, in Oxford, Ga.

The "Father of Lights" has but claim'd His own,
    And "our Charlie" has gone to rest.

On that cold, pale forehead, in silence now
    Shine the traces of innocence blest;
Like the sun's last rays on an iceberg's brow,
    Ere it sinks to its deep-sea rest.

But oh! the sighs and the groans and tears
    That circle the old hearthstone,
Where his sparkling eye, in those happy years,
    Had but brighter and brighter shone!

How lonely and still are the childish toys
    That lie on the shelf and floor!—
The sadd'ning mementoes of guileless joys
    Never, never to gladden us more.

But alas! they linger here in vain;
    The *spirit* that charm'd them's fled;
And our hearts shall yearn till they meet him again,
    With a starry crown on his head.

Enroll'd for the courts of a cloudless reign,
    Let the infantile prince sleep on,

Till the angel herald returns again,
   When the gloom of the grave is gone.

Then the virgin spirit shall come in light,
   With eternal youth its boon,
To ennoble the dust which we hide from sight
   Till it shines in the blaze of noon.

Then hush forever the murmuring tongue!
   For the morning of joy shall come,
And the family harp shall again, restrung,
   Resound in our heavenly home.

THE
World Without and the World Within,

BOTH SEEKING REPOSE.

Through all the vast domain of earth and of oceans,
   All nature submits to high Heaven's behest.
Her fearful and wild elemental commotions
   Are but struggles prelusive of ultimate rest.

The solid earth trembles—whole continents rocking
   With gases elastic pent up in her breast—
Till the heaving volcano, all barriers mocking,
   Disgorges its fires, and the globe is at rest.

The atmosphere, toss'd by the cyclone's gyrations,
   Bears death on its wings from the storm-brewing west,
Uprooting the forest, o'erwhelming plantations—
   Then pure, though exhausted, at last sinks to rest.

Old Niagara's flood, with no pow'r to restrain it,
   Tumultuous rolls to the steep, rocky crest;

Then with thunderous plunge leaves a rainbow behind it,
    And silently glides to the ocean to rest.

When regal ambition is fuming and tow'ring,
    And hosts rush to battle, their valor to test,
The red clouds of war, hurtling angry and low'ring,
    Are rent by artillery, and kingdoms find rest.

The doomed sons of labor, aroused by the morning,
    Have toiled through the sunshine, fatigued and unblest,
Till the bright starry millions, the heavens adorning,
    Have lighted them home and have lulled them to rest.

The man who has honored the God of creation,
    And striven through life for the realms of the blest,
As the storm-clouds retire—to his soul's exultation—
    Shall gaze on the rainbow, the token of rest.

This wondrous economy knows no cessation,
    But reigns under heaven, as the wisest and best.
Thus tempest, and tumult, and toil, and privation,
    Though ages should pass, are the preludes of rest.

But if earthquakes and cyclones and cataracts, yielding,
    Obey the decree to their natures address'd ;
Then, courage, my soul ! for th' Eternal is wielding
    The world's *moral* forces to crown thee with rest.

And when bliss sempiternal our senses engages,
    This truth—long by millions angelic confess'd—
Shall shine on forever, unmeasured by ages—
    That *service in heaven is the glory of rest.*

A Tribute to the Heroic Dead.

Written by request of the ladies of Oxford, Ga., to be sung on the occasion of strewing garlands upon their tombs, in the "Soldiers' Cemetery," May 1, 1867.

FAREWELL, heroic strangers!
   We weep around your tombs.
For us you fac'd all dangers,
   For us you met your dooms.

CHORUS.

No mother now can bless you,
   No father's presence cheer;
No loving wife caress you:
   You rest in silence here.

The storm of war has ended,
   The roar of battle ceased;
No posts are now defended:
   Their guards are all released.

Cho.—No mother now, etc.

The vernal flowers are blooming,
   And nature lives again,
While cheerless *winter's* looming
   Around our honored slain.

      Cho.—No mother now, etc.

But here, in grateful duty,
   Your mother's sex have come
To wreathe in fragrant beauty
   The soldier's lonely tomb.

      Cho.—No mother now, etc.

Forget you will we *never!*
   Where'er we rest or roam;
Your names shall live forever
   Where Freedom finds a home!

      Cho.—No mother now, etc.

A New Year's Reflections—1863.

LET PAST ILLS BE FORGOTTEN, AND FUTURE JOYS TRUSTFULLY ANTICIPATED.

ANOTHER year has fled and gone!
   Its buried millions sleep.
Its beggar'd orphans sigh alone—
   Its widow'd mothers weep.

The lurid storm that hurtled high,
   With vengeance on its wings,
Has fled; but left a gloomy sky,
   Where godless strife still rings.

Ten thousand tombless dead are there—
   Once heroes in the field—
And sorrow wails along the air,
   Where cannon-thunders peal'd.

The dim and distant past yet gleams
   In fitful light afar,

A NEW YEAR'S REFLECTIONS—1608.

While *New Year* pours its birthday beams,
   And lights its morning star.

Then why recall these months of pain,
   And re-enact their woes?
Must grief and tears forever reign,
   Though Heaven its smiles bestows?

Away! insurgent thoughts, away!
   In Lethean floods expire.
I hail with joy the new-born day;
   New themes my spirit fire.

A God surrounds the path I tread;
   His rainbow spans my sky;
His nameless mercies crown my head;
   His angel guards are nigh.

Then welcome each returning year,
   While light and love are given;
For when we close this brief career,
   Our life begins in heaven.

The Grandeur of Nature and the Glory of Grace, contrasted.

I have seen the sunlit mountain
   Bathing 'mid the clouds of spring;
I have heard the gushing fountain
   Loudly through the forest ring:

I have skimmed the boiling billow,
   'Twixt the ocean flood and sky;
When bright Phœbus sought his pillow
   'Mid the sea-nymphs' lullaby:

I have seen a peerless glory
   Arch the darkling front of heaven;
And have heard creation's story
   By the starry millions given.

And amidst these scenes of splendor,
   Filling earth and air and sea,
Oft my feelings homage render
   To the boundless Deity.

Still, oh still, I'm lone and cheerless,
　Till the reigning God appears;
Pours His light, and bids me, fearless,
　Triumph in this world of tears.

Mountain, rainbow, sun and ocean,
　Lose their glory in His blaze;
While my soul in deep devotion
　Sinks, enraptur'd with the gaze.

A Tribute of Gratitude.*

The day-star burned high over Mamre's broad plain,
  Flooding city and sea with his rays;
While its grand oaken forest subud'd his fierce reign,
  Shading Abraham's tent from their blaze.

Here the patriarch mused in his door, o'er the scene,
  While benevolence ruled his great heart,
As three gentle strangers approached on the green,
  With a message from Heaven to impart.

The patriarch rose, then in courtesy bowed,
  And welcom'd these guests to his home.

---

* When on a visit to the city of Baltimore, towards the close of the year 1868, the author was permitted to form the acquaintance of Mr. and Mrs. Broadbent, of that city, a noble, generous, and pious pair, with no lineal descendants to cheer their board and brighten their declining years, but whose open-hearted benevolence and Eastern hospitality were promptly and warmly extended to the ministerial *stranger*, who, shortly after his return to his own loved home in the South, penned this grateful tribute to his kind benefactors. Since that time Mr. G. Broadbent has been called to his reward. May Heaven's blessings attend his surviving consort!

To offer refreshments and rest he was proud,
    Unconscious that *angels* had come.

The fold and the garner were tax'd for their best—
    Eastern luxury crown'd the full board;
While the heralds angelic admir'd as they bless'd,
    Till in wonder he gazed and ador'd.

No angel, my host and my hostess, was there,
    When your halls were thrown wide to your guest,
A bright "*child of promise*" to pledge as your *heir*,
    In return for his comfort and rest.

'Twas a stranger, *earth-born*, whom you cherish'd and cheer'd
    At your princely and generous home;
But the patriarch's God, whom that stranger rever'd,
    Will reward you in years yet to come.

And when hoary hairs shall encircle your brows,
    And you're loaded with honors and years;
As he sinks to his rest, he'll remember his vows,
    And embalm your loved mem'ries with tears.

The war-god, in wrath, may have steep'd him in
    woes,
  And his home bear the scourge of his curse;
But a warm *Southern heart* ever gratefully glows,
  Till consign'd to the shroud and the hearse.*

---

*The war between the States had then closed, but its *sequences* were bearing heavily upon the author.

A Souvenir of Love.

Written by the author on a valentine sent to his beloved wife on the 14th of February, 1856, and while delivering his fifteenth course of Chemical and Pharmaceutical Lectures, in Augusta, Ga.

A "VALENTINE! a valentine!" delighted beauty cries,
As quick she breaks the ruddy seal, to feast her longing eyes.
She gazes on the honeyed lines, and drinks their nectar in,
Then binds the motto to her heart with jewel'd brooch and pin.

Dear wife, expect no burning strains, nor darts, nor turtle dove;
'Tis no enraptur'd swain indites this modest meed of love.
'Tis manhood's ripest fruit, matur'd by suns of passing years,
Most fragrant in the home that's blest with woman's smiles and tears.

One score and eight returning years have crown'd
    our nuptial ties,
And age has left its mild impress, to win us to the
    skies.
Ten thousand gifts indulgent Heaven has on our
    pathway pour'd,
And children stand like olive plants around our
    happy board.

Then, dearest partner of my youth, companion of my
    age,
Accept another pledge of love upon this virgin page.
In sweeter union let us taste the joys so richly giv'n,
And live in peace and love on earth, to live *again* in
    heaven.

The Ladies' Welcome.

A MASONIC ODE.

Prepared for, and sung by the pupils, before the members of the Grand Lodge of Free and Accepted Masons of the State of Georgia, with other members of the fraternity, at the Annual Commencement of the Southern Masonic Female College, in Covington, Ga.—an institution under the patronage of that Grand Body—June 20, 1871.

The winds of old winter have fled to their mountains,
    And summer has garnish'd the forests and skies;
While manhood and beauty have left hills and fountains,
    To grace this assembly with joy-beaming eyes.

CHORUS.

    Thrice welcome! ye sons of the sires of past ages;
        We bid you thrice welcome to these classic halls.
    The noble descendants of savans and sages,
        Your praise shall resound through our time-honor'd walls.

Through three thousand years have your altars been burning—
    Their soft, waxen lights beaming steady and clear.

Both in palace and prison — disloyalty spurning —
   You've reach'd the grand age when we welcome you here.

    Cho.—Thrice welcome! etc.

Hail! hail to the Temple on old Mount Moriah!
   Whose builders first rose to the gavel's shrill sound.
Its glories symbolic proclaim'd the MESSIAH,
   Whose truth has for ages your altar-tops crowned.

    Cho.—Thrice welcome! etc.

Thus pillar'd and stately, *Strength*, *Wisdom* and *Beauty*
   Sustain and adorn your blue, star-spangled dome;
While *Faith*, *Hope* and *Love*, in the *Ladder* of duty,
   All woo to the skies and a heavenly home.

    Cho.—Thrice welcome! etc.

Then hail, jewel'd Order! fair *woman's* protection;
   Her fast, faithful friend 'mid the dangers of life.
Her daughters, before you, with love and affection
   Will cherish your mem'ries, as maiden or wife.

    Cho.—Thrice welcome! etc.

Each summer return and make known, through your college,
That Masonry honors the child of her birth;
And the "Means" and the "Clio,"*twin sisters in knowledge,
Will wreathe you with flowers and sing to your worth.

    Cho.—Thrice welcome! etc.

---

* The two Literary Societies of the College.

Woman in Paradise, and Woman in Christendom.

In the safety of Almighty keeping,
   Surrounded by unreliev'd gloom,
A nebulous universe, sleeping,
   Lay hush'd in eternity's womb.

But a firmament's birth-time was nearing,
   To swell the bright host on parade;
And a new zone of worlds was appearing—
   For the mandate Divine was obey'd.

The grand panorama completed,
   Through decades of ages now gone,
By the anthems of angels was greeted,
   And its sun-lighted glories roll'd on.

Our young planet-home shone in splendor,
   With its oceans and mountains and plains,
While its groves rang with symphonies tender,
   Re-echoed in loveliest strains.

Though rich in the floods from its fountains—
    Unceasingly grand in their flow—
No MIND was enthron'd on its mountains,
    Nor rul'd in its valleys below.

But lo! the Eternal descended
    To garnish his new-born domain;
For his heaven and earth must be blended,
    And MAN must in majesty reign!

The harps of celestials resounded;
    The *monarch* illumin'd the scene;
The joy of creation abounded,
    And earth wav'd her banners of green.

How blissful the boon of existence
    Which open'd communion with *light!*
No cloud hung in gloom in the distance,
    And seraphs turn'd earthward their flight.

The soft, purple blush of the morning
    Gave way to the flood-light of noon,
The mountains and forests adorning,
    Till night claim'd the sheen of her moon.

The hosts of the firmament round her
   Did homage with banners unfurl'd,
And in silence rever'd Him who crown'd her
   Fair queen of a sweet-sleeping world.

No counterpart yet grac'd creation;
   Man, lofty and lone, walk'd abroad,
Or knelt in sublime contemplation,
   To adore his invisible God.

No pulse beat responsive around him;
   No features reflected his own;
To none kindred sympathies bound him—
   He stood in his glory *alone*.

But Jehovah ne'er wak'd an emotion,
   Nor sprung a high wish in the mind,
To tantalize love or devotion,
   And fade, to leave curses behind.

Oh no! ye bright ranks who adore Him,
   Emblazon'd with *truth* as ye burn,
Rise in glorified grandeur before Him,
   The foul imputation to spurn!

* * * * *

But nature, in beauty reposing,
   Ne'er sounded the deeps of his soul,
Till WOMAN, his eyelids unclosing,
   Pour'd ravishing bliss through the whole.

All radiant with angelic graces,
   She shone in the light of her God;
And her internal peace left its traces
   On cheeks ting'd with innocent blood.

Her beauty and purity blended,
   And, glowing with Heaven's *first* love,
Woke pæans of praise, which ascended
   To mingle with anthems above.

* * * * *

But the universe, blazing with glory,
   Turn'd *dark* o'er the first guilty pair;
For Lucifer, learning their story,
   Had pour'd *death* and *doom* on the air.

Oh weep, ye unborn generations!
   And Heaven's rich mercies implore;
For a curse follow'd hell's sinuations,
   And the "garden of bliss" is *no more!*

Thus from Eden, where angels first found her,
   Eve fled from the frown of her God;
Yet its odors, still clinging around her,
   Made fragrant the path which she trod.

   *   *   *   *   *

Fair exile! though banish'd and blighted,
   Still the loadstar and light of thy race!
Reserv'd, with the Godhead united,
   To open the flood-gates of grace.

Thy brow wore the impress of Heaven
   Through ages of guilt rolling by,
When the signal of mercy was given,
   And the "Star in the East" lit the sky!

Its bright sister millions surrounded
   And shone upon Bethlehem's plain,
While the broad empyrean resounded
   With "glory's" exalted refrain.

Hail! hail the Messiah, ye nations!
   The banner of "peace" is unfurl'd;
And by wondrous, sublime revelations,
   A VIRGIN *gives life to the world!*

   *   *   *   *   *

The Cross held its victim suspended—
   Earth shudd'ring in dread to the sky;
And with pangs—every muscle distended—
   The GOD-MAN was *struggling to die!*

Amazed, overwhelm'd and confounded,
   The petrified thousands stood by;
But, amid the doom'd throng who surrounded,
   Lov'd *Mary* and *John* caught His eye.

Oh! deathless and boundless affection
   For the *mother* who kissed Him at birth!
In His death-throes he vouch'd Her protection,
   And hallow'd *that name** upon earth.

Thus throned and exalted forever,
   The *cross* in her bosom enshrin'd,
Fair woman shall reign ever, ever,
   O'er the hearts and the homes of mankind.

Then hail! brightest type of creation!
   Though once overshadow'd by gloom,
Yet *now*, with a *world's* acclamation,
   Thy SON has brought *life from the tomb!*

---

* Mother.

Gloom and Glory;

OR,

THE DARKNESS OF *CONVICTION* CONTRASTED WITH THE LIGHT OF *CONVERSION*.

Nature groans when stunning thunder
   Cracks the scowling vault of heaven,
Riving mountain crags asunder,
   Down in headlong ruin driven.
But the storm-cloud's wildest clangor
   Softly dies upon the ear,
If an injur'd God, in anger,
   Stirs the trembling sinner's fear.

Deeply heaves the wailing ocean,
   Lash'd by madd'ning wintry storms;
Water-spouts, with whirlwinds' motion,
   Stretching high their specter forms.
Yet the raging seas are quiet—
   Hush'd to noiseless, dead repose—
When the penitential spirit
   Struggles with its weight of woes.

Change the scene! Aurora, coming,
   Heralds in the god of day.
Hark! the busy world is humming;
   Nations rise to greet his sway.
Yet how dim the sun of heaven,
   When compared to glory's light
Streaming on a soul forgiven,
   And in raptures at the sight!

Gorgeous glows the emerald mountain,
   Bath'd in light of vernal skies,
Crowning high yon crystal fountain,
   Garnish'd rich in rainbow dyes;
Yet how faint an adumbration
   Of the saints' eternal home!
Hallelujah! God's creation
   Shadows but the joys to come!

The Triumph of a Lofty Faith in Woman.

The following stanzas are intended as a feeble tribute to the memory of a departed friend—Mrs. AMELIA A. ANDREW—wife of the excellent and lamented Bishop JAMES O. ANDREW, of Georgia, who now rests with his sainted consort in heaven. In writing them, the author has but obeyed the promptings of his own heart.

Gifted with a mind of no ordinary caliber, largely developed and improved by an extensive acquaintance with human nature, Mrs. ANDREW was characterized by a high and dignified sense of propriety, in all her intercourse with others; by an unflinching firmness and steadiness of purpose in the greatest exigencies of life; and above all, by a sound and enlightened *piety*, which, though at one time severely tested, shed a heavenly luster around her dying bed, rarely equaled, and still more rarely surpassed.

SHE is gone! She is gone! I behold her now
   On the bosom of love reclining,
While the cypress and rose on her marble brow
   Are in lovely embrace entwining.

How fiery and fierce was the battle wag'd,
   As she near'd her approaching heaven!
Perdition exhausted its fruitless rage,
   And its last red bolt was driven.

Still heavenward and high as she pitch'd her flight,
   Her infernal foes surrounded,
Till, scath'd by the blaze of supernal light,
   They cower'd, and fled confounded.

Then, pois'd on the wing of a lofty faith,
   With the power of prayer around her,
She smiled, and courted the parting breath
   To sunder the ties that bound her.

Serenely calm as the land-lock'd bay
   When the far-off storm is sweeping,
Her waveless soul in the sunlight lay
   Like the smile of an infant sleeping.

"No tear at my tomb," said the dying saint,
   As her raptur'd soul ascended;
"Let the song and shout—not a cheerless plaint—
   Be in heavenly triumph blended."

But her hour had come! 'Twas a hallow'd sight!
   For an angel throng attended;
And lost in the blaze of immortal light,
   Was her bright career thus ended.

What a moment was that when her heaven had come,
   And the Godhead's glow surrounded!

When welcoming millions receiv'd her home,
    And eternity's harps resounded!

Farewell, then, my sister!—a long farewell!—
    Though your form and your words may leave us,
That affectionate grasp of your dying hand
    Will never depart—believe us!*

All, all shall be well, though a husband sighs,
    And your motherless babes are weeping;
You have taught them to trust in the God of the skies,
    And they're safe in His heavenly keeping.

O God! to the friends of our sister gone,
    Let *her* conquering grace be given;
And then, when the drama of life is done,
    We shall greet her again in heaven.

---

* Shortly before her departure, sitting upright in her bed, and holding the hand of the writer with an ardent grasp, her face radiant with a superabundant revelation from on high, she said: "Doctor, I am going to leave you; but *you have a long time to live yet.*" Nearly *thirty years* have since elapsed, and *that* friend, after so many years of heavy intellectual and physical toil, still *lives!* grateful to God for his protracted life, and for the health, strength, and privilege yet allowed him, to proclaim that everlasting gospel which has eternized the bliss of Sister ANDREW, with millions more, in heaven.

A Farewell Souvenir.

Addressed to Mrs. Jane W. Baldwin, *the daughter of an old and esteemed friend of the author, namely,* Rev. Thomas Samford, *and presented on the eve of her departure, with her husband, for Louisiana.*

How fitfully varied the stream of life!
    How strangely capricious it wanders!
Ev'ry curve of the current with change is rife,
    Where the good man prays and ponders.

You are borne on its bosom, my dear young friend,
    Away to the land of strangers;
May Mercy and Truth their resources blend,
    To succor your soul n dangers.

Farewell, then, Jane! may your home be bless'd
    By the smiles of approving Heaven;
And your light still shine in the far, far West,
    Till your home in the skies is given.

And when I am called to my rest above,
    And your children learn the story,

Oh teach them to cherish my name in love,
    Till we meet in the realms of glory.

And now farewell to your honor'd sire!
    No more upon earth I'll meet him;
But aloft, in the land of the harp and lyre,
    By the grace of God I'll greet him.

And when old age shall our strength destroy,
    And mem'ry fails before it,
We'll each call the name of his own *dear boy*,
    And remember *him who bore it*.*

---

* The Rev. T. Samford had a son called after the author, who gave the name of that venerable man to one of his own sons, at the baptismal font.

Young Womanhood Ripe for Heaven.

A TRUE SKETCH FROM THE LIFE AND CHARACTER OF

MISS SALLIE L. MEANS,

The Priceless, Sainted Daughter of the Author.

On December eleventh, eighteen fifty-one,
When the bleak blasts of winter were fast coming on,
A sweet little stranger appeared in our room—
Its face like a rosebud beginning to bloom.

A mother's embrace soon encircled her child;
She looked on in rapture, and gratefully smiled.
In its soft flannel wrapper it lay on her breast—
She kissed its plump cheek, and soon lulled it to rest.

In its bright, happy smile and its tender blue eyes,
Like a sunrise in May, under welcoming skies,
A *father* beheld his own dear flesh and blood,
And, bowing in pray'r, gave his infant to God.

That trust—ne'er recalled—was recorded in heaven,
And her soul in young childhood to Jesus was given.

Oh blessed alliance of innocent youth,
In holier bonds than Naomi's with Ruth.

While the sweet, lowly violet peeps from the lawn,
To greet the first sunbeams that purple the dawn,
The dahlia and sunflow'r, ambitiously bold,
Display to the noonday their crimson and gold;

So, in life's early morn, as her knowledge increas'd,
And the bright Sun of Righteousness rose in the east,
As he cleared the horizon she caught his first gleams,
Content with the fragrance inhaled from his beams.

Like her own *fav'rite* flower,* she bloomed in the shade,
Nor envied the "Bon Ton," in splendor arrayed.
As well feed the famished with diamonds and pearls,
Or deck fair Minerva with jewels and curls.

From the smiles of her Saviour no charms could allure;
She reached noble womanhood modest and pure.
Clear and calm as the lake when it sleeps in repose
Was her innocent breast, where no wild passions rose.

---

* The violet.

Joy beamed from her eyes, and Love molded her heart,
While the Graces combined every gift to impart.
Her charity, boundless, embraced her whole race;
It was heaven-born, glowing, and shone in her face.

Her dear "Orna Villa "* was bright where she moved,
And her presence was balm to the hearts that she lov'd.
Her song cheered the parlor, and rang through the hall,
And her kind voice of " welcome " was tendered to all.

She was born from on high; her affections were there;
And her heart's aspirations found converse in pray'r.
On the heavens and earth she delighted to gaze,
And her deep adoration was mellowed to praise.

Her filial devotion, inspired from above,
Was profound and intensive, and radiant with love.
Blest trait of the household! how sweetly displayed,
When parents are honored, revered and obeyed!

---

* Her father's residence.

The young clustered round her in Sunday-school
 hours,
As rosebuds half-blown, under green, shady bow'rs;
To her bland, soothing voice, charmed attention was
 given,
As she fondled, caressed them, and woo'd them to
 heaven.

The white tents of Jacob, how goodly and grand
They rose on her eye, as they spread o'er the land!
But the dearest of scenes on the path which she
 trod,
Were the carbuncled gates of the Zion of God.

Its portals stood wide, her approaches to greet,
And its courts rang with melodies, hallowed and
 sweet.
This luminous center attracted her soul,
For there the Shekinah shed light through the whole.

But adieu, holy hour, never more to return!
Bright visions now gone! and in sackcloth we
 mourn.
Though her *spirit's* in heaven, her *dust's* in the tomb,
And the home of her childhood is mantled in gloom.

Thus lustrous with virtues, and buoyant and blest,
Her life glided smoothly, and all was at rest;
Till a dark, lurid cloud up her sky seemed to creep,
And a deluging cyclone whelmed all in the deep.

But light shone around her as danger drew nigh,
And, embraced by her Saviour, she feared not to *die*.
"*All's right!*" was her watchword, with dying lips given,
And an angelic escort convoyed her to heaven.

Like the crystaline snow-flake, the child of the skies,
That descends pure and spotless, to ravish all eyes;
But warmed by the sunbeams, and winged for its flight,
It heavenward soars, and is lost to the sight.

Farewell, thou sweet phantom of purest delight!
Evanescent and faded, yet "*all, all is right!*"
But in regions of bliss, God of love, let us meet,
In the noontide of glory our sainted to greet!

A Poetic Offering

TO THE MEMORY OF MRS. MARTHA ELIZABETH McINTOSH,

(FORMERLY GRIGGS), OF MICANOPY, EAST FLORIDA.

Another life-struggle is ended,
   And victory rings on the air;
Another bright spirit's ascended,
   'Mid tear-drops, and praises, and pray'r.

Her wing, when the death-knell resounded,
   Was spread for her heavenly flight;
Invisible angels surrounded,
   And rob'd her in vestments of light.

In the home of her childhood she listen'd
   To whispers of *peace* from above;
They told in the pearl-drops that glisten'd
   In eyes beaming kindness and love.

Transported with raptures supernal,
   She long'd for her rest in the sky;
And tendered a farewell eternal
   To pleasures that bloom but to die.

Soon her maidenly graces and beauty
    Threw charms o'er a thrice happy home;
And our bride vied in conjugal duty
    With the lovely Lucretia of Rome.

A *rosebud* of ravishing sweetness
    Now hung from the green parent stock,
When the storm came with hurricane fleetness,
    And bore off the gem by its shock.

But as sunshine succeeded to shower,
    O'er dear Ella's motionless form,
Three plants freshly bloom'd in the bower
    But recently drench'd with the storm.

The dove o'er the deluge was flying;
    The Ark was at rest upon high;
The floods in their basins were lying,
    And happiness beam'd from her sky.

Install'd as a wife and a mother,
    Her home was a temple for prayer,
A prototype fair of *another*,
    Unclouded by sorrow or care.

The glorious *Volume of Ages*
    Was thron'd on the heights of her soul,
And reign'd, through its life-giving pages,
    With blissful and boundless control.

No godless assemblage e'er found her
    Polluting her heaven-born caste;
While Infancy nestled around her,
    And Poverty smiled as she passed.

But alas! when the day-king's descending—
    His mantle all jewel'd with light—
And the tints of the rainbow are blending,
    It is but the prelude of night.

So, too, the convolvulus, blooming
    In rosy luxuriance at morn,
Soon droops, by the noon-heat consuming
    The beauties with which it was born.

While the sun-beaten flocks are reclining,
    And rivers dry up o'er the plain,
It sleeps till the dew-drops are shining,
    Then blushes with morning again.

Thus faded our dear, sainted sister—
Full blown—in her womanly prime,
But sank, as her little ones kiss'd her,
To bloom in a lovelier clime.

Emory College and Oxford Apostrophized.

A PERORATION TO AN ADDRESS DELIVERED BEFORE THE Φ. Δ. Θ.* SOCIETY, NOVEMBER 21, 1873.

Then hail! ye old halls, in whose sylvan retreat
The young of the land all in harmony meet!
A college of Christians, where God is enthron'd,
And "free love" and folly are scorn'd and disown'd.

These nurselings that cling to thy bosom to-night,
And imbibe from thy paps intellectual might,
Will, in forthcoming years, when enlaurel'd by Fame,
Their old "Alma Mater" with plaudits proclaim.

Dear Oxford! thy shady recesses invite
To build up the soul and to crown it with light.
From thy pure, hallow'd homes, vulgar vices are driven,
And woman, sweet woman! allures us to heaven.

---

*Φιλια Δεκτη Θεο, "Friendship is pleasing to God."

Apostrophe to an Album,

DEDICATED ON THE WEDDING-NIGHT.

LOVELY page! thou long hast slumber'd,
    Robed in stainless virgin white.
Other scrolls their days have number'd;
    Life begins with thee to-night!

Bridal love has sought and found thee,
    Brilliant type of woman's grace!
Vestal lamps are blazing round thee,
    Joy illumes each shining face.

Long, oh long, sweet Album! cherish,
    Bright with smiles or moist with tears,
Thoughts and names which ne'er shall perish,
    'Mid the tide of rolling years.

Bid the beauteous bride remember,
    When all mem'ries else decline,
One bright eve—the *eighth November*,
    Eighteen hundred forty-nine!

Brief, at best, the trust assign'd thee—
   Bearing gems from saint or sage;
Future search shall fail to find thee—
   Lost amid the wastes of age.

But when all thy heart-born treasures
   Shine no more to living eyes,
Those who scann'd thy sheets with pleasure,
   Still shall *live* when nature *dies*.

The Silent Power of Woman.

ADDRESSED TO MISS LEILA OGILBY, OF MADISON, GA.

There is power in the dew-drop that sleeps on the plain,
    When, rous'd by Aurora, it mounts to the sky;
For, stunn'd by its thunders and drench'd by its rain,
    Earth groans from her caves as the tempest rolls by.

So soft, gentle *woman*, the heart's purest joy,
    Excites men and nations to emprize and war.
One beautiful Helen fires Athens and Troy,
    And hosts bleed in battle, led on by her star.

There is power in the sunbeam that steals from the skies,
    And floods sea and mountain, unconscious of toil;
Awak'd by its dawnings, the world's millions rise,
    And store in their garners the wealth of the soil.

Thus noiseless, diffusive and brilliant *she* shines,
    Whose smiles bless the nations her presence illumes;
Exalts human nature, rude manhood refines,
    Gives statesmen their laurels, and heroes their plumes.

There is power in the zephyr that lulls us to sleep,
    When it moves in the whirl of the cyclone at sea;
Then marshals its thunders, and, ruling the deep,
    Whole navies are pow'rless to fight or to flee.

O woman, dear woman! the dew of the soul,
    The light of the homestead, the breath of old age!
Thy sanctified nature the world shall control,
    For thy kiss on the *infant* gives fame to the *sage*.

Then, Leila, sweet girl, for an empire prepare,
    Whose scepter is *love*, and whose legions are *smiles;*
Thy subjects all *heroes*, who honor the fair;
    Thy realms **a** *bright domain*, unmeasur'd by miles.

A Glacier in the Heart;

OR,

PHLEGMATIC BEAUTY ETHEREALIZED BY GRACE.

[THE Aurora Borealis is supposed to be the result of electric emanations from the immense fields of ice which cover the polar seas—passing off in brilliant coruscations of diversified hues towards the zenith, becoming less and less distinct, until lost in the higher and rarer regions of the atmosphere. Although more frequently witnessed in high northern latitudes, yet within the last half century several of these magnificent pageants have adorned our southern skies.]

  How rich and soft yon crimson glow
    That tints the Arctic skies!
  While bleak and wide, outstretch'd below,
    An icy ocean lies.

  'Tis but the transient flush of light
    The polar iceberg flings;
  Yet crowds admire the lovely sight,
    Unthinking whence it springs.

Fit emblem of the roseate tide
    That flushes beauty's veins;
While o'er the *affections*, far and wide,
    Eternal *winter* reigns.

The eye may flash with intellect,
    The cheek mock painter's art;
Yet Heaven's transpiercing gaze detect
    A *glacier in the heart.*

But oh! when fervent grace is *felt,*
    Transcendent beauties rise;
Affection's gelid waters melt,
    And rainbows span the skies.

Love hallows all the sacred scene,
    And woman dwells in light;
Her eye, her smile, her life's serene,
    And angels hail the sight.

As glowing tints far west appear,
    When twilight shades begin,
Thus, soft and beautiful and clear,
    Her evening skies shut in.

The Little Pine Cupboard that Stands by the Wall.

THE following rustic verses were composed by the author in his private moments, to commemorate an epoch in his domestic life, connected with many associations which gave rise to some tender reminiscences of other days. The metrical arrangement was suggested by that popular old ballad, "*The Old Oaken Bucket that Hung in the Well.*"

YE muses immortal, your song-tribute bring!
What muse for dear Oxford would scruple to sing?
Fair Erato, come, with thy roses and lyre,
For plaintive contralto our genius inspire.
Though humble the theme, hear a devotee's call,
To sing the old cupboard that stands by the wall.
    The nice, cozy cupboard—the genial old cupboard—
The life-giving cupboard that stands by the wall.

Come, wing our conceptions and roll up the past
As thistle-down flies on the breath of the blast.
Bid Story present us, in picturesque forms,
The scenes of the hamlet—its calms and its storms;

And in clustering conclave its subjects install
Round the honor'd old cupboard that stands by the wall.
   The hoary old cupboard—the peerless old cupboard—
The grandmother's cupboard that stands by the wall.

    *   *   *   *   *   *

We sing, then, a husband and blooming young wife,
Just fresh from the altar, launch'd out upon life.
No luxuries crown'd their pretensionless home;
With peace round their hearthstone they long'd not to roam.
But time brought a *nurseling* to chirrup and crawl,
With a *mouth* for the cupboard that stood by the wall.
   Then a sweet little cupboard—a bright, shining cupboard—
A dear, darling cupboard, that stood by the wall.

With calm resignation they met woe or weal—
The man at his pill-box, the wife at her wheel.
Contented and cheerful, they hopefully toil'd;
No vaulting ambition their heritage spoil'd.
Full rich with the wealth of their snug cottage hall,
And the well-plenished cupboard that stood by the wall.

A tidy young cupboard—a full-bosom'd cupboard—
The cream-flowing cupboard that stood by the wall.

Thus years roll'd away, and more prattlers appeared,
All piously taught and all pray'rfully rear'd.
With filial affection they kiss'd the kind hand
That molded their souls to the great and the grand;
While, loaded with comforts and cheer for them all,
Was the tempting old cupboard that stood by the wall.
　The oft-courted cupboard—the plentiful cupboard—
The luscious old cupboard that stood by the wall.

But industry prosper'd, and rosewood was seen,
With rich broider'd damask of crimson and green;
While music swell'd high through the carpeted room,
Evolv'd by the touch of young beauty in bloom.
But always the same—far removed from them all—
Was the voiceless old cupboard that stood by the wall.
　The canny old cupboard—the closeted cupboard—
The old-fashioned cupboard that stood by the wall.

But oh! when the household had circled the board,
And a sanctioning blessing from Heaven implor'd;

When babyhood hungered, or fretted, or cried,
These claims reach'd the *pantry*, and all were supplied.
Fast friend to the needy, and waiting their call,
Was the princely old cupboard that stood by the wall.
    That kindly old cupboard—the food-laden cupboard—
The bounteous old cupboard that stood by the wall.

When war spread its havoc and blasted the land;
And famine, gaunt famine, with blade and with brand
Fill'd graves by the thousand, where armies had striv'n,
And sent burning homes in red cinders to heav'n;
Still hoarding its stores for its mistress's call,
How priceless that cupboard that stood by the wall.
    The cheerful old cupboard—the teeming old cupboard—
The provender cupboard that stood by the wall.

Its finger-worn button, *yet* faithful and true,
Still guards all its treasures, and hides them from view;
It holds in its bosom, delf, porc'lain and plate,
And honors the landlady early and late.
When appetite clamors and threatens a brawl,

'Tis hush'd by the cupboard that stands by the wall.
    The gentle old cupboard—the soothing old cupboard—
The peace-making cupboard that stands by the wall.

Now forty-four winters have whiten'd their locks,
They shine in the sunbeams like snow on the rocks;
Their children and grandchildren make the house ring
With laughter and noise, as they frolic and sing.
Then quitting their sports, upon "grandma" they call,
And rush to the cupboard that stands by the wall.
    The tireless old cupboard—the patient old cupboard—
The fast-waning cupboard that stands by the wall.

Quaint steward of the household, we've long liv'd together,
And breasted the onsets of wind and of weather;
But, soulless and silent, thou sheddest no tears,
Though husband and wife are now bending with years.
Yet, till they're consign'd to the hearse and the pall,
They'll bless the old cupboard that stands by the wall.
    The dingy old cupboard—the crazy old cupboard—
The age-furrowed cupboard that stands by the wall.

Thou shalt linger awhile with their offspring to dwell;
But oh! where's the seer that shall dare to foretell
When thy moth-eaten panels shall rot in the mire,
Or thy splintered remains shall be food for the fire?
Yet children unborn shall thy mem'ry recall,
And mourn the old cupboard that stood by the wall.
   The little pine cupboard—the cherish'd old cupboard—
The time-honor'd cupboard that stood by the wall.

Farewell, then, companion and friend of our youth!
Thou faithful exponent of goodness and truth!
Soon, soon we'll be destin'd forever to part—
A long separation of cupboard and heart.
But to Sallie, "our Sallie," with its treasures and all,
We leave the old cupboard that stands by the wall.
   Our Sallie's own cupboard—the long belov'd cupboard—
Her *mother's* old cupboard that stands by the wall.*

---

* Their beloved daughter, Sallie Leonora, the intended heiress of this treasured relic, "the old cupboard," was called to her *rest* before her father or mother.

The Farewell and the Greeting;

OR,

THE OLD YEAR AND THE NEW — 1865 AND 1866.

Our Internecine War Having Closed in 1865.

'T<small>IS</small> the silence of midnight ! The year's at its goal,
  In the star-lighted arch of the sky ;
And a hemisphere sleeps, from equator to pole,
  As the wave-tide of ages rolls by.

While the earth is in dreams and the heav'ns are at rest,
  And creation moves on as of yore,
Eternity's offspring falls back on her breast,
  And the year *Sixty-five* IS NO MORE !

As a bubble, afloat on a sunlit wave,
  Shines a moment in purple and green,
Then breaks on the brow of its ocean grave,
  And is lost in the boundless scene ;

So *its* fleet golden hours have but flash'd and fled
    O'er the wastes of the ages past;
Not an obelisk marks their oblivious bed—
    Not a stone where they breath'd their last.

Yet the deeds of men, with their smiles and tears,
    In eternal, changeless light,
Shall burn o'er the tombs of departed years,
    When the sun is quench'd in night.

Oh the scenes! the scenes that have met the eye,
    In the rush of the rolling year,
To be canvass'd again, when a God draws nigh,
    And the judgment thrones appear!

For alas! there are regions of damning crime,
    That send up their stench on high,
Provoking the bolts of the wrath sublime
    On the guilt of the year gone by.

There lust and mammon their curses pour
    Upon heads and hearts and homes;
While murder and perjury reek with gore,
    And tremble till vengeance comes.

Yet the beauty of Virtue and charms of Grace
    Bring the angel of mercy near,
While Religion and Science, in holy embrace,
    Start afresh on their bright career.

But a birth! a birth from the womb of night!
    Lo, an *heir* of the old year's born!*
And the welcoming heavens, all rob'd in white,
    Shall herald the news to the morn.

Old Arcturus smiles from his azure throne,
    And pledges a peaceful reign;
And Orion, begirt with his starry zone,
    Leads on in the royal train.

O'er a waking world, at the opening day,
    Loud shouts from the million ring;
As the day-god rolls on his cloudless way,
    And the birds of song take wing.

Young Hope sits thron'd on the brow of youth,
    And kindles its sparkling eye;

---

* At midnight.

And Piety girdles her loins with truth,
    To strike for her crown on high.

E'en the widow is flush'd with a transient joy,
    By the blaze of her warm hearthstone,
As she hugs to her bosom her orphan'd boy,
    Nor would forfeit his love for a throne.

Now the world's busy thousands to new toils spring,
    With a bounding, conquering zeal,
While cities resound with the whirl and ring
    Of the spindle, the hammer, and wheel.

Then why should our Zion deplore the past,
    Or boast of her triumphs won?
Let her warn the world with a trumpet blast,
    And *shout when her work is done!*

The nations are rous'd to the claims of God—
    All Christendom lends her aid;
The harvests are white, and the fields now nod
    To the stroke of the reaper's blade.

The smoke and the storm that with thunder-tone,
    Overswept our battalions slain,

Are the clouds and darkness that shroud His throne,
  But to blazon His wider reign.

Though a continent rock under bursting bombs,
  And millions of missiles fly,
As legions, led on by the roll of drums,
  Are hurrying on to die,

Still glory's ahead of this dark campaign,
  And Emmanuel's empire's nigh;
For a grander nation shall grace His train,
  And shine in the bright'ning sky.

When the sun shall have near'd the burning line,
  To light up the earth and heaven,
The war-god's spear shall have ceased to shine
  On the fields where the brave have striven.

Ere the peach shall have blush'd in an August sun,
  Or the vintage have grac'd the vine,
Our Union shall tow'r over Goth and Hun,
  Like a giant refresh'd with wine.

Then away, away on this bright *New Year*,
  With the shout and the song of love!

Fill the courts of God with the boundless cheer,
  Till it blends with the hymns above!

And oh! when December's last lone star
  Shall have pal'd in the light of the morn,
May the *new-crown'd Year*, from his blazing throne,
  Shed a splendor on hosts unborn!

The Triumphant Wife and Mother.

Dedicated to the memory of Mrs. Callie L. Smith, *consort of* Rev. L. M. Smith, D. D., *President of the Southern University, Greensborough, Ala.*

There is death in the air, and there's gloom in the heart,
When husband and consort are destin'd to part;
When loveliness lies on the verge of the grave,
A household in tears, and no power to save.

But, dear Rev'rend Brother, *stand fast,* and *rely!*
There is peace in her heart, and there's heav'n in her eye.
Her wings are outspread—she must leave thee alone:
A few panting breaths, and the angel *is gone!*

* * * * *

There's rejoicing above, in the realms of the blest,
As their millions look out for the new wedding-guest;
For glory awaits her, Mount Zion's in sight,
And her wide, golden gateway is flooded with light.

She stands on its threshold—then flies to embrace
Her glorified Lord, who has sav'd her by grace—

Then rises to visions and raptures untold,
As eternity's glories begin to unfold.

Farewell, then, dear Callie! now sainted and seal'd,
For the heav'n of thy faith is in splendor reveal'd;
We must weep o'er thy dust, and lament for our loss,
But shall trust for *re-union* through Christ and His cross.

The bedroom is empty, the parlor's in gloom,
But thy virtues have left there a long, rich perfume.
A *mother's* sweet voice, and the smile of a *wife*,
Thy children and husband shall cherish through life.

Community mourns o'er the breach in its ranks,
And the churches unite in hosannas and thanks,
That God fills the chamber whence saints take their flight,
With faith, love and joy, as they're borne from our sight.

Hail, hail, then, the scene that advancingly looms,
Where the "lov'd and the lost" are new-born from their tombs;

Where the Lord's ransom'd hosts roll their songs
    through the skies,
And the GREAT EVERLASTING pours bliss from His
    eyes!

Rapt myriads stand round the *"Ancient of Days,"*
And the universe rings with their anthems of praise.
How boundless the pageant! how endless the strain,
When the LORD OF REDEMPTION is scepter'd to
    reign!

Oh bear us aloft, blessed Spirit of Love,
Through the gloom of the grave to our mansions
    above,
Where the saints of all ages, the purchase of blood,
Shall welcome us home to the bosom of God.

To an Itinerant Minister's Wife.

Oh why dost thou lodge in the house of the stranger?
   And why far remov'd from thy innocent joys?
Oh why dost thou roam over regions of danger,
   Where fell marsh miasma its thousands destroys?

Forgive, oh forgive me! no longer I wonder;
   I see in thy husband a herald of God,
From Zion proclaiming, in language of thunder,
   The curse and the cure through Immanuel's blood.

Go, go then, my sister, and warmest affections
   Shall welcome thee on in thy mission of love;
Go comfort and cheer him, and share that protection
   So solemnly pledg'd from thy Father above.

Thus harmless the changes of life shall roll round thee,
   So long as thou lovest like beautiful Ruth;
Not the fearful alarum of death shall confound thee,
   For peace crowns the faithful that *die* for the truth.

An Infant's Flight to Heaven.

CHILD OF HON. T. M. AND MRS. ANNA NORWOOD, OF SAVANNAH, GA.

Go, sweet spirit, infant stranger,
   Join the cherub throng on high;
Fly this world of doubt and danger—
   From its tears and terrors fly.

Angel forms approach to meet thee;
   Soft they kiss thy life away;
Heaven's redeem'd in rapture greet thee
   Welcome to eternal day.

Doting mother, cheerless bending
   O'er that blasted, breathless frame,
Upward gaze—thy babe's ascending!
   All that's left the grave may claim.

Faith recalls the melting story
   Of the Son's vicarious blood;
Points to chariots bound for glory,
   Lights dear "Manson" home to God.

Beauty Enhanced by Piety.

ADDRESSED TO MISS ISABELLA HAYES, NOW MRS. S. THOMAS, ATHENS, GEORGIA.*

Oh say, dost thou see, o'er the dark purple wing
   Of the far-distant storm-cloud, the rainbow of peace;
As, gorgeously rob'd in the sunlight of spring,
   It smiles on the world till the show'r-drops cease?

Brighter far, Isabella, the radiance that beams
   From the soft soul of beauty, *illum'd from on high*.
With a luster undying, its mellow light streams
   O'er the storm-beaten pathway that leads to the sky.

No gloom shrouds its splendor, no years dim its rays,
   Life's toils and misfortunes are lost in its blaze;
It burns high and holy, through death's angry flood,
   Then shines on forever with angels and God.

Great Sun of the universe! Light of the spheres!
   Grand luminous center of matter and mind!
Thus lovely and pure, when Messiah appears,
   May my friend *of the Album* her paradise find!

---

*Written in Miss H.'s Album.

A Morning in May.

'Tis an hour of sweetness in balmy May,
    When swallows are out on the wing;
They twitter in joy as they skim away,
    To welcome the opening spring.

The jay-bird, clad in her tunic of blue,
    Pipes clear on the passing breeze;
In his crimson robe flaunts the red-bird too,
    As he sings to the listening trees.

The leaping lambkins, in sportive mood,
    Are curveting round their dam,
Or daintily cropping their verdant food
    By the side of the lordly ram.

From the dimpling stream, in its winding flow,
    Where the sauntering herd now graze,
The silvery perch, from their beds below,
    Leap up to their Maker's praise.

The mellowing showers from genial skies
    Have freshen'd the lawn and field;
The landscape blooms in a thousand dyes,
    And foretokens the harvest yield.

All nature's alive with the thrill and flush
    Of a new-born, bounding life;
Sweet strains from her grand orchestra gush,
    And the tumult of joy is rife.

The earth, with its blendings of light and shade,
    Now glows with the smile of God,
Adumbrating scenes of a nobler grade,
    In the fields beyond the flood.

Surely heaven has more than earth can boast,
    For our longing, bounding souls!
For *Nature*, with all her starry host,
    No wounded heart consoles.

O Mighty Creator! these gifts of grace—
    Mere drops of exhaustless love—
Are shower'd abroad on a thankless race,
    To win them to thrones above!

Oh yes! there are glories beyond this goal,
    Surcharg'd with the love of God!
Then soar on the wings of faith, my soul;
    They are *thine*, through atoning blood!

The Sear Leaf.

DEDICATED TO THE HON. JOHN P. KING, OF AUGUSTA, GA.

Dear generous friend of the auld lang syne,
    Our decades are hast'ning away;
But the joys of the past, still lingering, shine
    Like the sun at the close of day.

The burden and heat of the day we've borne,
    And have tasted its weal and woe;
We have learnt from the past to rejoice and mourn,
    And to ponder the path we go.

But each has been blest round his own hearthstone
    By a wife's and a mother's smile;
Oh, what earthly gift from the Father's throne
    Can so sweetly the heart beguile!

As the ivy clings to the old church-wall,
    And encircles its tottering tow'r;
Or mantles with verdure the antique hall,
    To grace it in sunshine or show'r;

Thus filial affections, as manhood fades,
    To the ancestral homestead cling;
They delight to repose in its evergreen shades,
    And to cherish the mem'ries they spring.

Our names must live in the age to come,
    When the *father* is lost in the *son*,
And the dutiful heir of the lonely home
    Shall illustrate the sire that's gone.

    *   *   *   *   *

Thus the grand panorama of life moves on,
    But on earth there are boons from heaven;
And when virtue and truth have the victory won,
    There's a crown to the conqueror given.

There are triumphs to win in the empire of thought—
    In the boundless domains of the soul—
Unsounded by trumpet, by gold unbought,
    And untrac'd upon tablet or scroll.

Let these stir ambition to strike for the skies,
    To conquer corruption and sin;
And Faith, Hope and Love shall in glory arise,
    And light up the temple within.

Mont Blanc looks down from his throne of rocks,
    With his diadem wreath'd of snows;
On his sides, deep cleft by convulsive shocks,
    There the "Rose of the Alps" still blows.

Thus heaven-born greatness sublimely looms
    Over passions that bluster below;
Though disasters may blight, moral loveliness blooms,
    And the flowers of Paradise grow.

Then roll, ye fleet years, to eternity's verge!
    But oh, bear us on to our rest;
And then, at life's close, let the funeral dirge
    Be exchang'd for the songs of the blest!

Friendship's Memorial.

FOR MRS. M. S. KING,

THE AMIABLE CONSORT OF HON. JOHN P. KING, OF AUGUSTA, GA.

Oh, who can stay the rolling spheres,
   Or lock Apollo's wheel?
Who, who arrest the flight of years,
   Or future life reveal?

Dear honor'd friend of other days,
   My heart could but rejoice
When first I learnt to love and praise
   Your noble husband's choice.

A lovely bride you stood confess'd,
   In beauty's flush and glow;
No griefs to rend your tranquil breast,
   Some thirty years ago.

The world was fresh, and friends caress'd,
   While wealth and pleasure pour'd

Their ample stores to make you bless'd,
    And crown your cheerful board.

But oh! the fell destroyer's blade
    Has ravag'd unrestrain'd;
The cypress casts its deadly shade
    Where light and pleasure reign'd!

How many bounding, joyous souls,
    That grac'd your parlor floor,
Have reach'd their dreamless, silent goals,
    To smile and bless *no more!*

The writer, then in manhood's prime,
    With clear and cloudless eye
Look'd out on life, while hope sublime
    With rainbows spann'd his sky.

* * * * *

But why recall "the lov'd and lost,"
    The pains and sorrows past?
Why wail our land by tempests toss'd,
    To swell the vengeful blast?

Still, life is ours, and nature smiles;
    Her seas and mountains stand;

Her peaceful rule the heart beguiles,
    And gladdens ev'ry land.

But higher still, in light enthron'd,
    The reigning King appears;
The Godhead has for guilt aton'd,
    And mercy calms our fears.

Old age is nurs'd with heav'nly care,
    Gray hairs with glory crown'd;
Angels the dying couch prepare,
    And viewless hosts surround.

The good and pure shall ever find
    New bliss for joys entomb'd;
A hallow'd peace to soothe the mind,
    And light where darkness gloom'd.

Then, honor'd friend, though childhood's past,
    Our youthful luster fled,
And setting day is hast'ning fast,
    There's sunrise just ahead!

May gracious Heav'n unfold the day
    To all our raptur'd eyes,
And bear us, with our friends, away
    To bliss beyond the skies!

The Golden Girdle.

The girdle is an indispensable appendage to the dress of an oriental, and is employed to tuck up and secure the long flowing vestments worn in the East; thus affording greater freedom of locomotion, and at the same time bracing and supporting the waist, the weakest portion of the body, where the spinal column stands alone, without the auxiliary aid of any surrounding bony structure. This girdle, among persons of rank, is, even at the present day, made of the most costly fabrics, luxuriously ornamented with the precious metals and garnished with brilliant dyes. The symbolic representation of the "Son of man, clothed with a garment down to the foot, and girt about the paps with a *golden girdle*," as detailed in the glowing language of the Apocalypse, was probably anti-typical of the costume of the Jewish high priest, and emblematical of *regal* as well as of *sacerdotal* dignity. The golden girdle worn by that consecrated functionary was connected and probably woven with the ephod; the latter ornament consisting of "gold, and blue, and purple, and scarlet, and fine twined linen," and richly embroidered; while the *girdle* was wound in graceful folds twice round the body, crossing the pectoral or breastplate in front; and at this point of interjunction were inserted twelve precious stones, upon each of which was engraved the name of one of the tribes of Israel. As St. John the Evangelist has declared that the saints are "made *kings* and *priests* unto God," the poetical appropriation which we have made of the "golden girdle," in the few stanzas which follow, may not, we trust, be regarded as alien to the divine authority.

8*

In this dark world, which bears the frown of God—
    Where nature heaves beneath His blasting curse,
Where sin has pour'd its desolating flood,
    And whirls its victims on to ills far worse—

Still there's a *hope*, that paints the Christian's sky,
    And sheds its luster on his trusting soul;
Still there's a *faith*, that lifts its gaze on high,
    And stands unmov'd where rifting thunders roll.

Still there's a *tie*—a priceless, golden tie—
    That binds pure spirits to th' eternal throne.
We foil hell's cunning, and its strength defy,
    When holy love encircles with its zone.

Then let the sickly world disgorge its hate,
    And languid friendship freeze upon the lip,
Let beggar'd virtue quit the halls of state,
    And bloated vice her poison'd chalice sip;

Let time's resistless waves still murmur on,
    And whelm their millions under tides of years;
Let earth, convuls'd with torture, reel and groan,
    And vent her throes in hot volcanic tears.

Let lurid lightnings rend the vault of heaven,
    And howling tempests scourge the trembling world;
Mad oceans lash the clouds, by thunders riven,
    And stone-girt mountains from their seats be hurl'd.

Let nature's death-knell ring in Gabriel's blast,
    And startled millions leap from sod and sea;
Wild floods of flame engulf the globe at last,
    And shrieking ghosts in vain red vengeance flee.

'Midst these astounding scenes, where courage dies,
    Where none's secure but he whom God defends,
This golden cincture's known throughout the skies,
    And brings that succor which the Godhead lends.

Loud hallelujahs leave my bounding heart,
    And sound the triumphs of redeeming blood;
He that would harm me, hence, with hellish dart
    Must rend the *girdle*, or DETHRONE A GOD!

A Pledge of Affection,

TO VICTORIA A. MEANS, SECOND DAUGHTER OF THE AUTHOR.

Written when from home, on St. Valentine's Day.

WILL my daughter, in years yet to come,
   On this valentine wistfully gaze?
Remember her sweet Oxford home,
   And the scenes of her happy young days?

And when her gay childhood is o'er,
   And she blooms in the ripeness of age,
Let a time-honor'd *father* once more
   Bless his child, from this beautiful page?

A Madrigal.

TO HIS OLD FRIEND, DR. H. GAITHER,
OF OXFORD, GA.,
ON HIS PRESENTATION OF A MAGNIFICENT PEACH TO THE AUTHOR.

THANKS, thanks for the gift of your "Nonpareil" peach,
   So large and so luscious, so soft and so rare;
Were Hesperian gardens at all within reach,
   I'd shrewdly suspect you a favorite there.

Who'd growl at his fortunes, or envy renown,
   As its exquisite nectar outvied the *first* kiss?
What lady would ruffle her brow by a frown,
   While her palate was sated with sweetness like this?

But richer by far, in the gardens on high,
   Hang the rich, golden clusters the world underrates;
A feast for the *soul*, and a feast for the *eye*,
   Of the millions who enter its gem studded gates.

Girlhood Expanded to Womanhood:

LINES WRITTEN IN A NEW ALBUM,

Presented by the Author to Miss Elizabeth Luckie, *of Covington, Ga.*

Those sweet, simple accents which first charm'd my ear
In the hours of your childhood, I still seem to hear;
But the laughing blue eyes and the soft flaxen hair
Of the light-hearted Lizzie, oh, where are they?—where?

Does my vision deceive? Sure I trace in that face,
In that mild azure eye, and that womanly grace,
Her I rock'd on my knee, in her own happy room,
In her father's full strength and her mother's full bloom.

And when *we* shall close our returnless career,
And that sweet smile of love be exchang'd for a tear,
Then remember, dear girl, to the faithful 'tis given,
That their lost friends on earth shall rejoin them in heaven.

And as years roll away, and the lov'd ones you knew
Gently pass to the skies, like the bright morning dew,
Kindly glance at this page in the still hour of pray'r,
For a *friend* of your childhood shall meet with you there.

Poetic Paraphrase of the Forty-eighth Psalm.

(Verses 2, 12, 13, and 14.)

How beautiful Mount Zion stands,
  Confronting Northern skies;
Her sacred heights the world commands,
  And fills the nations' eyes.

On old Moriah's sunlit wing
  Her glorious temple shines;
There God, within, her reigning King,
  Unfolds His great designs.

Oh, walk about her spacious courts,
  Go round her tower'd walls!
Eternal rock their strength supports,
  And grandeur fills her halls.

Mark well her bulwarks' massive size,
  And fix your thoughtful eye
Upon her palaces, that rise
  In splendor to the sky.

Let babes be told of Zion's fame,
　　Let age its off'rings bring,
That children's children may proclaim
　　Her everlasting King.

The God who crowns her hills with light
　　Is ours forever more;
Till death He'll guide our feet aright,
　　And teach our souls t' adore.
　　　8✶✶

The Young Student's Cloudless Close of Life.

Lines suggested on witnessing the morally sublime scene exhibited in the triumphant death of Mr. Maximilian W. Kendall, *a student of Emory College, Georgia, and the* first *who was ever summoned to the tomb from the rolls of that Institution. He was a member of the Methodist Episcopal Church, and a young man who promised much to the Church and the world.*

The bolt is sped, and the whizzing string
   Is the dirge of its victim sounding.
He *falls!* but in death he is crown'd a king,
   The foe of his life confounding.

A month ago, and his manly form
   Was seen in the strength of beauty;
With vigorous step and affections warm,
   He mov'd in the sphere of duty.

Science was pouring her morning rays,
   Foretok'ning a noon of splendor;
And Eloquence loan'd her witching lays
   To insure the heart's surrender.

How wide the field to ambition's view!
   How alluring the scenes before him!

But, sav'd by the God that his *father* knew,
    He lov'd, and liv'd to adore Him.

His soul, baptiz'd with the life of God,
    Had scorn'd unholy pleasures;
The Cross illumin'd the path he trod,
    And on high he stor'd his treasures.

How hallow'd the scene as his end drew nigh!
    A glow from the Godhead descended;
It sat on his lip, and it fir'd his eye,
    As if heaven and earth were blended.

Thus, far away from the stormy wave
    O'er the soul of the guilty driven,
He stood on the verge of his early grave,
    In the cloudless light of heaven.

Away, away from the scene of death,
    Where pray'rs and tears are pouring,
His spirit mounts up on the parting breath,
    And ascends to God adoring!

He's gone! he's gone! he's ascending now;
    An immortal choir surround him,
And a halo encircles the marble brow,
    In the chamber where they found him.

Messiah's Coming Reign.

A SUNDAY-SCHOOL MELODY.

Our banner's unfurl'd !
There is hope for the world,
And the foes of the Cross from their heights shall be hurl'd.
Christ's reign has begun,
And the world must be won,
And millions redeem'd ere the campaign is done.

CHORUS—REPEATED.

Then triumph and sing
To our conquering King,
Till island and ocean with peans shall ring.

The bright Morning Star
Is now seen from afar,
Nor pales in its splendor in peace or in war.
But the day-beams appear
From the sun in its rear,
And Zion shall bask in the blaze of his sphere.

CHORUS—REPEATED.
Our churches now ring,
As our little ones sing,
And swell the loud anthem, "Messiah is King."

Youths flock to His arms,
Overcome by His charms,
And, lock'd in His bosom, are free from alarms.
CHORUS—REPEATED.
Our fathers may die
'Mid the holy war-cry,
But the old flag of Zion shall still float on high.

Their helmet and shield,
To their children they yield,
And the next generation shall shout on the field.
CHORUS—REPEATED.
No longer bow'd down,
Let us strike for the crown,
And win for the Cross everlasting renown.

Through faith in His blood,
Let us follow our God,
In the paths which apostles and prophets have trod.

CHORUS—REPEATED.

Neither carnage nor blood,
Nor famine nor flood,
Shall cloud the bright reign of Immanuel-God.

How blissful the scene,
When the soul sits serene,
Entranc'd in His presence, with no veil between.

CHORUS—REPEATED.

Hallelujahs shall rise
To the God of the skies,
As the Shiloh, descending, shall ravish all eyes.

Then valley and plain,
And mountain and main,
Shall swell the grand chorus and roll on the strain.

CHORUS—REPEATED.

Then triumph and sing,
To our conquering King,
Till island and ocean with peans shall ring.

The Minister's Farewell.

The following lines were written by request, and designed for a young minister who was about to take leave of his congregation, brethren and friends, to enter upon another field of labor. They were mainly intended, therefore, to be used as a solo.

How swiftly the years of our pilgrimage fly,
As weeks, months and seasons roll silently by;
Our days are soon number'd, and death sounds our knell;
We scarce know our friends till we bid them *farewell*.

The righteous and wicked move slowly along,
In crowds, to the tomb, both the old and the young;
The *good* rise to heaven, the *bad* sink to hell!
They take, on life's verge, an eternal *farewell*.

O God! are the nations all bound for the tomb?
Must the godless and guilty soon meet their dread doom?
Save! save, great Redeemer! oh break the sad spell!
Forgive, and prepare them to bid earth *farewell*.

Farewell, fellow sinners! We're free from your blood;
Our message deliver'd, we leave you with God.
We've begg'd and persuaded, but cannot compel;
Till the great day of doom, then, we bid you *farewell!*

Oh! think on the scenes which await you in death!
The cold clammy sweat, and the quick panting breath;
The winding-sheet, coffin, and slow-tolling bell—
Your last, solemn, fearful, *eternal farewell!*

To you, fellow Christians, I turn with delight.
The grave cannot harm you; your prospects are bright.
Be faithful and humble; temptations repel;
You'll soon leave the world with a smiling *farewell.*

Farewell, then, my brethren! in body we part,
But one common Saviour unites us in heart;
Through grace we will conquer the world, flesh and
    hell,
And then bid this earth a triumphant *farewell.*

Farewell to its labors! farewell to its cares!
Its thousand misfortunes, temptations, and snares!
We'll mount on faith's pinions, with angels to dwell,
Where saints never hear the sad, *parting farewell!*

"Little Ones, My Little Ones."

NO. I.

A PARODY UPON "MARYLAND, MY MARYLAND," A BOHEMIAN AIR.

A SUNDAY-SCHOOL HYMN.

Supposed to be sung by the Principal and Teachers, in concert with the School.

EMMANUEL reigns from shore to shore,
    Little ones, my little ones;
    Little ones, my little ones;
And though our land be drench'd with gore,
Like Syria's plains in days of yore,
His chariot's at our temple door,
We'll trust His grace forevermore,
    Little ones, my little ones.

Our Father hears our warm appeal,
    Little ones, my little ones,
While on our native soil we kneel,
    Little ones, my little ones;
For life and death, for woe and weal,
Our penitential vows we seal,

And trust in God, and not in *steel*,
    Little ones, my little ones.

Our spotless banner spurns the dust,
    Little ones, my little ones;
The sword *we* wield shall never rust—
    Little ones, my little ones;
Then shun old Balaam's sordid lust,
Learn faithful Joshua's holy trust,
And rise and reign with all the just,
    Little ones, my little ones.

Come! 'tis the lovely Sabbath day,
    Little ones, my little ones;
Come, lay your childish toys away,
    Little ones, my little ones;
With Mary's spirit, mild as May,
With Abr'ham's faith in active play,
Oh, come to praise, and come to pray,
    Little ones, my little ones.

Come, for your hopes are bright and strong,
    Little ones, my little ones;
Come, for your absence does you wrong,
    Little ones, my little ones;

Come mingle with this happy throng,
That love their Saviour all day long,
And swell His praise with ringing song,
    Little ones, my little ones.

Dear children, break wild passion's chain,
    Little ones, my little ones;
The blows you strike are not in vain,
    Little ones, my little ones;
Rejoicing hosts shall join your train,
And "heav'n, sweet heav'n," your loud refrain,
Shall millions echo back again,
    Little ones, my little ones.

With sparkling eyes and blushing cheek,
    Little ones, my little ones;
With joyous spirits, pure and meek,
    Little ones, my little ones,
Our song shall rise from week to week,
From hill to hill, from creek to creek,
From southern shore to mountain peak,
    Little ones, my little ones.

And when the Sabbath bell shall toll,
    Little ones, my little ones,

No idler shall our steps control,
    Little ones, my little ones.
Should fire and flood their fury roll,
And battle rage from pole to pole,
We'll worship God, and save the soul,
    Little ones, my little ones.

Hark! hark! how sweet this infant hum,
    Little ones, my little ones;
More thrilling far than fife or drum,
    Little ones, my little ones;
'Twould stir the souls of deaf and dumb.
We're marching to our heavn'ly home :—
Hail! angels, hail! we come, we come,
    With little ones, *our* little ones!

"Sunday-school, our Sunday-school."

NO. II.

ADAPTED TO THE AIR OF THE PRECEDING HYMN, NO. I.

A Sunday-school Antiphony.

SUNG BY PRINCIPAL AND TEACHERS.

THE Sabbath bell has sweetly toll'd
    For Sunday-school, our Sunday-school;
The little lambs are in the fold,
    At Sunday-school, our Sunday-school.
Their humble names are all enroll'd
In lines of richer tint than gold;
Their shepherd's eye they here behold,
    At Sunday-school, our Sunday-school.

SUNG BY THE PUPILS.

Thrice welcome, then, this lovely day,
    For Sunday-school, our Sunday-school;
How bright the scenes we here survey,
    At Sunday-school, our Sunday-school.
Six days are past in work and play,
Since last we met to praise and pray;

Oh! who'll consent to stay away
    From Sunday-school, our Sunday-school?

The godless world ne'er thinks nor cares
    For Sunday-school, our Sunday-school;
It cannot vend its tempting wares
    At Sunday-school, our Sunday-school;
But many a child, that rudely dares
To touch its bribes and risk its snares,
Is lost, for want of weekly prayers
    At Sunday-school, our Sunday-school.

But, shelter'd here, we'll gladly stay
    At Sunday-school, our Sunday-school,
Within our little land-lock'd bay,
    In Sunday-school, our Sunday-school.
The ocean waves may wildly play,
Lash'd on by tempests, night and day;
We're safe from danger, far away
    At Sunday-school, our Sunday-school.

Our teachers dear, whose guidance wise,
    At Sunday-school, our Sunday-school,
Has train'd these lambkins for the skies,
    In Sunday-school, our Sunday-school,

In death must shortly close their eyes,
And at the resurrection rise,
To join us in immortal ties,
    From Sunday-school, our Sunday-school.

Our fathers soon shall meet no more
    At Sunday-school, our Sunday-school;
Their holy counsels soon be o'er
    At Sunday-school, our Sunday-school;
I hear the distant Jordan roar,
As fast they near its sounding shore—
We'll soon, with tears, their loss deplore,
    From Sunday-school, our Sunday-school.

SUNG BY TEACHERS AND PUPILS, STANDING.

Then, children, let us rise and sing,
    At Sunday-school, our Sunday-school;
Our richest off'rings let us bring
    To Sunday-school, our Sunday-school;
Our spirits now are on the wing,
We're mounting to our Shepherd King,
Where hallelujahs long shall ring,
    From Sunday-school, our Sunday-school.

"Live for the Skies."

A CAMP-MEETING HYMN.

ESPECIALLY DESIGNED FOR THE YOUNG OF THE LOVELIER SEX.

WRITTEN DURING THE LATE DISASTROUS WAR.

DEAR YOUTH, in the glory of life's happy morning,
   The world blooming bright in your innocent eyes,
When the rainbow of hope is your heavens adorning,
   Embrace your Redeemer, and *live for the skies.*

For soon the horizon may darken before you,
   Disease may assail and temptations surprise,
While the wretch may deceive who has sworn to adore you—
   Then cling to the Cross, and still *live for the skies.*

The dear, sainted mother, that kiss'd and caress'd you,
   Has gone to her rest, where the soul never dies.
How lonely the home where she counsel'd and bless'd you!
   Then hallow her mem'ry, and *live for the skies.*

That chivalrous father, whose arms now enfold you,
   May sink on the field, amid loud battle-cries,
And sleep far away, never more to behold you—
   Then lean on the Saviour, and *live for the skies.*

While o'er our encampment bright angels are bending,
   With palms in their hands and with love in their eyes,
And the grace of salvation's from heaven descending,
   Oh, kneel at these altars, and *live for the skies!*

Oh, strike for a region that's free from illusion,
   Where hearts never throb and where bliss never flies;
Where the waters of life flow in sparkling profusion,
   And *man lives forever with God, in the skies!*

The Sound of the Gospel is Passing Away.

The sound of the gospel is passing away—
  The days of probation are ending;
Oh, who will return to the Saviour to-day,
  While the prayers of His saints are ascending?

The sound of the gospel is passing away,
  Long, long has it linger'd around us;
How sweetly in childhood it taught us to pray!
  But, alas! we are still where it found us.

The sound of the gospel is passing away,
  That rose on the wings of the morning,
When the dear, dying sire, call'd his offspring to pray,
  And bequeath'd them his last solemn warning.

The sound of the gospel is passing away—
  It rolls over island and ocean;
The Kaffir and Hindoo are learning to pray,
  And bow in their souls' deep devotion.

The sound of the gospel is passing away—
    It flies on the four winds of heaven;
Creation now dawns with millennial day,
    And the world's final warning is given.

The sound of the gospel is passing away,
    The offers of mercy are closing;
Ten thousands are gone who've refus'd to obey,
    And are now under tombstones reposing.

The sound of the gospel is passing away—
    Soon, soon shall the great work be over,
And the grave hold its dead till the last burning day
    Shall the doom of creation discover.

The sound of the gospel is passing away—
    O God! ring its last notes in thunder!
Let peal after peal rouse the sinner to-day,
    To fly from the wrath he is under.

The sound of the gospel is passing away,
    And bearing the saints to their glory;
Hail, mighty Redeemer! Oh, when shall thy sway
    Bring the millions of earth to adore Thee?

The sound of the gospel is passing away,
　　The skies with the Godhead are bending !
Oh, shout, ye redeem'd, for the darkness is day,
　　And the glorified hosts are ascending !

Sparkling Beauty Transient.

TO MISS TELLULAH Y****.

The cascade that leaps from the mountain,
    And echoes your beautiful *name;* *
As it winds far away from its fountain,
    Soon forfeits its title to fame.

So beauty and youth in high places,
    That noisily flash on the eye,
Lose the charm of young life, and its graces,
    When age robs the cheek of its dye.

---

* See Appendix D.

Paternal Affection.

TO THE AUTHOR'S ELDEST DAUGHTER, MARY E. P. MEANS.

Dear Mary, remember your father's affection,
    Who smil'd o'er your cradle and silenc'd your fears;
Who threw round your childhood his grateful protection,
    And gave you to God amid prayers and tears.

And when with the burden of years he is bending,
    Or messenger angels have borne him above,
Oh then, my dear child, while a tear-drop's descending,
    Let this little valentine whisper his love!

The Wedding Ring.

TO MRS. DR. JAMES N. SIMMONS, ATLANTA, GA.

Away, away on your bright career,
    For the wedding-ring has found you
Away, amid smiles and bridal cheer,
    With the arms of love around you.

Now enter the checker'd scenes of life,
    Where the smile and tear are blending;
Heaven's richest boon is a *lovely wife*,
    Whether weal or woe's depending.

Then live, dear Lizzy, to bless your home!
    'Tis the noblest boon of beauty;
Let affection grave on your honor'd tomb—
    "*She knew, and she did her duty.*"

Camp-meeting Song.

A TWELVEMONTH more has roll'd around
Since we were on this tented ground;
Ten thousand scenes have mark'd the year
Since we last met to worship here.

Relentless Death has hurl'd his darts,
And lodg'd them deep in noblest hearts;
O'er old and young, in ev'ry sphere,
He's triumph'd since we worship'd here.

But we are spar'd! To Heav'n be praise!
Our God has lengthen'd out our days;
We've left our homes with hearts sincere,
And met once more to worship here.

Ye hosts of Israel, lowly bend,
And let your hearts in pray'r ascend;
That Heav'n may lend a list'ning ear,
And answer while we worship here.

Return, ye wand'ring souls, to God;
He claims the purchase of His blood.
Oh, loathe your sins, to Christ draw near,
And seek Him while we worship here.

Dear mourners, raise your tearful eyes;
Look heav'nward, and behold the prize!
Your Saviour smiles; renounce your fear,
And trust Him while we worship here.

Gird all the Christian armor on,
And nobly strike till vict'ry's won;
Our God shall guard the front and rear
Of all who humbly worship here.

The battle's strife will soon be o'er,
And war-worn vet'rans toil no more;
On Zion's heights we'll soon appear,
And no more meet to worship here.

The sinner's Friend we'll then adore,
Where tents are pitch'd to strike *no more;*
A glorious heav'n with angels share,
And *live,* and *love,* and *worship there.*

The Golden Wedding.

AN EPITHALAMIUM.

Gratefully celebrated on the return of the Fiftieth Anniversary of the wedding-day of the author and the partner of his earthly fortunes, formerly Miss S. A. E. Winston—*December 25, 1877.*

THE nuptial lamp is lighted now,
   The Christmas fagot burns;
The night of *fifty years ago*
   In memory returns;

When bright and strong the writer stood,
   In manhood's early spring,
And blooming beauty by his side.
   First wore the wedding-ring.

But oh! the change, the mystic change,
   Along the line of years!
Ten thousand griefs come trooping up,
   To melt his eyes to tears.

The youth, transformed, is now a sage,
 His raven locks are gray;
And vig'rous manhood, worn with toils,
 Shows signs of sad decay.

His blushing bride now stoops with age,
 The rose to ashes turn'd;
She bows to Heav'n, but, weeping still,
 Her "lov'd and lost" are mourn'd.

Departed joys in ghostly forms
 Come welling up to view,
Till present blessings urge their claims,
 And spring her faith anew.

Though half an hundred years have gone,
 Our grateful hearts adore
That Love whose countless mercies past
 Inspires our trust for more.

Still life, sweet life, is ours t' enjoy,
 With bright'ning hopes of bliss,
And children's children crowd to share
 The Golden Wedding kiss.

But some are gone! Their angel forms
   Now range th' Elysian fields,
Enrob'd with white and crown'd with stars,
   Which heav'n, exhaustless, yields.

Dear sainted *four!* in bliss live on;
   We ask not your return;
But oh! to meet your presence there
   Our raptur'd spirits burn.

Dear, faithful sons and daughters still
   Surround the old hearthstone,
And smiling friends their presence give
   To cheer the pilgrims on.

O Father! long vouchsafe Thy gifts!
   Make bright our evening skies!
Help us to close a faithful life,
   Then heavenward bid us rise!

Then, then farewell, a long farewell
   To sorrow, sighs and tears;
Emmanuel's smile is glory gain'd,
   Unquench'd by floods of years.

Our Golden Wedding's festal night
    Shall ne'er on earth return;
But heaven to happier scenes invites,
    Where souls shall never mourn.

There, in the cloudless realms above,
    Shall richer feast be given—
"*The Marriage Supper of the Lamb*"—
    Its guests, the saints of heaven.

We come, O Lord, by grace we come,
    Eternity to spend,
And celebrate *that feast* of love
    Whose sweets shall never end!

Appendix.

Appendix A—page 12.

The junction of the Arve with the Rhone furnishes a romantic and picturesque scene. The Arve is a furious torrent, born from the sides of the towering Col de Balme, and fed by the melting snows and ice of that majestic mountain. By its rush and abrasions down the steeps of those wild regions, it rapidly accumulates *detritus*, which, mingling with its frothy and foaming current, gives it the appearance of a river of creamy mud. At their point of junction, the impetuous Arve drives the pellucid waters of the Rhone to one side, and they refuse, for some time, to commix with the turbid flood; but are ultimately overcome, lose their transparency, and disembogue their common sedimentary mass into the bosom of the placid lake: a beautiful illustration of the contaminating and depraving influence of confirmed vice over unsuspecting and unguarded virtue. with which it may be thrown in contact.

Appendix B—page 12.

When on a visit, some years since, to the beautiful suburban residence of the ecclesiastical historian, Dr. Merle D'Aubigne, situated directly upon the margin of the lake, that distinguished divine and scholar said to the author, that he supposed the azure hue of the water was but a reflection of the blue color of the overhanging skies. Now this solution seems altogether unsatisfactory; first, because it should not retain its hue when the heavens are overcast with clouds—whereas that circumstance effects no change in its color. Second: the skies in Italy are quite as blue as those over Switzerland, and no such signal phenomenon is there noted. The writer therefore must seek another explanation, and attributes the color of the lake to the presence of iodine, brought down by its tributary streams from the iodiferous regions of the Alps, and chemically combining with fecula, or starch—a proximate principle common to nearly all vegetables, and found especially in their roots and tubers, and which the same regions abundantly supply. The starch, when in contact with the iodine—both being held in solution—strikes the characteristic blue tint, so well known to chemists, and so finely represented in the waters of Geneva.

APPENDIX C—PAGE 24

THE STONE MOUNTAIN is a huge and almost anomalous projection of solid Syenitic Granite, shooting up in solitary grandeur from an extensive outcrop of the granitic stratum which extends from New England through New Jersey, Maryland, Virginia North and South Carolina, and Georgia, terminating near the Tombigbee River, in Alabama. Its base approaches within one half mile of the Georgia Railroad, and is seven miles in circuit. Its elevation has been reported by Mr. George White, in his "Statistics of Georgia," at 2,226 feet above the small creek which runs near its base. It is inaccessible on all sides save one. The northern exposure presents an almost unbroken mural precipice of perhaps 1,000 feet in height. Altogether, it strikes the eye of the traveler as a grand, solemn, naked, and unique geological monstrosity, which has arrested the gaze and commanded the attention of admiring thousands—standing, as it does, in the midst of widespread and luxuriant forests and cultivated fields, and forty miles remote from the Kenesaw Mountain, the nearest considerable elevation, and one of the spurs of the Alleghany range.

APPENDIX D—PAGE 205.

The Rapids or Falls of Tellulah, so called by the Indians, are situated on the river of that name, within twelve miles of Clarksville, Habersham County, Ga., and may be properly ranked among the greatest natural curiosities of the United States. We furnish a brief sketch of this magnificent waterfall, by making a few " excerpta " from the published report of an intelligent friend who visited the spot and witnessed the scenery.

" The river," says the writer, " passes through a range or ridge of mountains for more than a mile, forming for its bed an awful gulf, and for its banks stupendous fronts of solid rock, like those of Niagara just below its great cataract, and of the Genesee river below the fall in that stream, a few miles above Lake Ontario. The height of the banks varies from 200 to 500 feet perpendicular. There are four perpendicular pitches of water, from 50 to 80 feet each, besides a great many small cataracts or cascades of from 10 to 20 feet in fall. The entire plunge, therefore, may be estimated at about 300 feet. The river, however, varies from 15 to 100 feet in width. These cliffs, combined with the foaming, roaring, bounding, impetuous current of water, exhibit novelty, beauty, and grandeur in the highest degree. This majestic scene lies in a wild, uncultivated and sterile region, on which the hand of Art has never laid its transforming touch, to soften or degrade, although now surrounded by an intelligent and thriving population."

After the sublime exhibition, thus imperfectly described, Tellulah's fame is *gone*, and the little river unites with its sister stream, the Chattoogo, from the north-east, and loses its name and its honors in their joint successor, the Tugaloo, together constituting the head waters of the beautiful Savannah, which, after a course of about 250 miles, disembogues in the Atlantic Ocean 18 miles below the " Forest City."

www.ingramcontent.com/pod-product-compliance
Lightning Source LLC
Chambersburg PA
CBHW031827230426
43669CB00009B/1249